CO

FORWARD

GET RID OF

MR. REALISTIC V: POPULARITY

KEEPING IT REAL V: MYTH

DEAR CARNIVAL

OUR DUTY AND JOB

ARE YOU A BAD MAN

CHANGE OUR BEHAVIOR

PARADISE GONE

NOTHING

USE TO BE GRIMY

NO EXPIRATION DATE

SUBMISSION

HEAVY ARTILLERY

OUR STORY

NATIVE BORN

G ANGELS

THREATENING OUR PATHWAY

POWER IN MOTIVATING PEOPLE aka P.I.M.P.

187 IN THE VIRGIN ISLANDS

187 II

CHEATING

STILL CHEATING

MORE CHEATING

INSIGHT

LIFE

NEWS FLASH

FORWARD

To whom it may concern, in the 21st century of the unknown the Ourstory Recorder aka V. I Hit Factory will stake his reputation and artistic greatness on this book, "The Real True Taughts of Good Over Evil" because the time has come to start promoting and supporting the Creator's original plan which is, "Good will conquer Evil and Love will triumph over Hate" and to make sure following the Laws of Creation becomes everyone's top and highest priority in life. The Creator has blessed my pen with the power and energy of telling like it is, without any sugar coating which is called "REALITY" aka TRUTH or FACT. So only the Creator instructs the Ourstory Recorder, no one else.

So, ALL HAIL GOOD OVER EVIL AT ALL TIMES.

Always remember the Ourstory Recorder's thoughts are never broken.
P.S. Thank you DJ Avalanche for blessing me with the turn up name of the V.I. Hit Factory, who is always batting 1000 with no strike outs.

Always, SUPPORT YOUR OWN TO THE FULLEST!!!

Mr. Dave R. Queeley
CEO/ Founder Reel to Reel Productions
MOTTO: Reel to Reel Is Real!!
05-13-2014

GET RID OF
By
Mr. Dave R. Queeley

The time has come for We the People to make the positive move and choice to GET RID OF the mind boggling and the ticking time bomb of extinction that will be caused by the new Hannibal Lector called BLACK ON BLACK CRIME. Life is not getting any easier, it's time to get up off our ass and start doing better in life and stop all the mental and spiritual lynching that continues to happen every time one of those senseless, random and unnecessary killings and shootings that take place in our communities and neighbourhoods. It's We the People do our duty and job to make the commitment to changing and reforming our communities and neighbourhoods that are now marked by deep iniquities and hatred, which are now slowly rotting them away.

The people who are the enemies of having manners, respect, love and good intentions for one another are an embarrassment to the game of life knows if you want to hate MAHOGANY PEOPLE, you kill them before they are born, especially the males; that's what PLANNED PARENTHOOD is all about. Especially the ones who are giving out free abortions on a daily basis. They are getting the job done of killing off the MAHOGANY PEOPLE, the unwanted people. ABORTION is the number one and BLACK ON BLACK CRIME is the number two killer of MAHOGANY PEOPLE around the world as we move forward into the abyss of the unknown. They have killed more people than any war and diseases put together. This is real talk, no sugar coating.

Extinction is forever, so always beware of these enemies of Good over Evil. The people who are involved with BLACK ON BLACK CRIME has forgotten back in the good old days of ONE GOD, ONE AIM, and ONE DESTINY, We the People had all the gold and diamonds and the enemies of manners, respect, love and good intentions for one another had all the Bibles aka The Good Book. Now in the 21st century, We the People have all the Bibles aka The Good Book and the enemies of manners, respect, love and good intentions for one another now have all the gold and diamonds.

In the 21st century having manners, respect, love and good intentions for one another is perceived as evil and not right at all because We the People have shown no indication we are ready and willing to halt BLACK ON BLACK CRIME which has been a source of mental and spiritual tension for the people for years who have no morals, values and integrity in their lives. There is no across the board consciousness in our communities and neighbourhoods that BLACK ON BLAK CRIME must end before it's too late and the ticking time bomb of extinction goes off for real. BLACK ON BLACK CRIME always has a negative impact on truth seekers efforts of trying to bring mental and spiritual peace, stability and unity back into our communities and neighbourhoods.

Our communities and neighbourhoods needs no more short lived solutions, but need long term solutions that will make sure they are victorious in the battle of Good over Evil. There is a lot of sadness and misery inside We the People's mind. body and soul caused by BLACK ON BLACK CRIME, but we will never raise a while flag in the battle of Good over Evil trying to GET RID OF BLACK ON BLACK CRIME. We have to remember no one is helping or extending their hands to help us fix this evil social ill and problem that is now a ticking time bomb to extinction.

We the People cannot continue to fear retribution from the fake thugs who are committing these senseless, random and unnecessary BLACK ON BLACK killings and shootings in the 21st century. We the People's message and warning to fake thugs is WE ARE READY AND WILLING TO SAVE LIVES and STOP THEM FROM TAKING A LIFE EVERYDAY THAT GOES BY. Life is too damn short to be playing with it like you're a fool. It's our duty and job to stay alive and stop BLACK ON BLACK CRIME. These feelings, attitudes and actions only keep the evil mentality of "greed is good" and hatred alive in our communities and neighbourhoods which needs to be destroyed ASAP.

"Greed is good" and hatred has turned some people into evil and gluttonous individuals who will do anything for the love of money, even take a life for no good and godly reason under the sun, moon and stars. The root of BLACK ON BLACK CRIME is not a recipe for happiness and a joyous existence in the world. It's a lesson in the harsh realities of the world, that if these evil feelings, attitudes and actions continues, extinction will soon be upon the people like a bad rash. We the People have to become individuals who are cool, calm and collected about exuding SELF assured love, respect and confidence far beyond the enemy's imagination.

Manners, respect, love and good intentions for one another know no nationality and fears no evil. It's time for the graduation of We the People from BLACK ON BLACK CRIME and free ourselves from the mental and spiritual captivity of injustice and darkness aka planned doom once and for all, by being a part of the Creator's original plan and following the Laws of Creation until prophecy is fulfilled in the future. The Walls of Jericho cannot hold We the People back if we decided to return to having manners, respect, love and good intentions for one another once again in our communities and neighbourhoods. When this starts to happen, BLACK ON BLACK CRIME will not continue to prevail and cause things to get worse for the people who are MAHOGANY.

The only way to GET RID OF BLACK ON BLACK CRIME, "GREED IS GOOD" AND HATRED IS FOR ALL MAHOGANY PEOPLE TO LOOK INSIDE!!

ALL RIGHTS RESERVED
12-31-2013: HAPPY OLD YEAR

Read on The Avalanche Radio Show on 01/08/2014

MR. REALISTIC V: POPULARITY

By

Mr. Dave R. Queeley

Mr. Realistic's immense popularity with the truth seekers is not a fluke. His popularity and success as a writer will always be a blessing from the Creator; because if you have a talent and don't use it for the betterment of society, the Creator will take it away. Each oratory shows the genuine feelings Mr. Realistic injects into his writing has been responsible for why he is so popular among the in crowd of truth seekers. The writings are real and at the same time, it has a universal message of having manners, love, respect and good intentions for one another which are offsprings of the Creator's original plan and Laws of Creation.

Anyone who reads his writing will understand his message that GOOD WILL CONQUER EVIL and LOVE WILL TRIUMPH OVER HATE. Mr. Realistic is now a triple threat all the way. A freedom fighter author and most of all a political activist for doing what's right for the people who are now suffering from mental, economical and spiritual slavery and being oppressed on a daily basis. Everyone loves a winning team. The team of Mr. Realistic, THE COMMON SENSE MOVEMENT, and the truth is just that…A WINNING TEAM. I bet if you join this team, it will be an inspiration.

Truth seekers have stopped blaming the world for their problems. They know they are the problem and they are the solution all balled up into one. You choose which one you want to be a part of; the problem or the solution. The choice is yours, to be good or to be evil. It's time to light our inner lamps and show the world that having manners, respect, love and good intentions for one another are the missing ingredients in life. In the future Good will defeat evil and take its rightful place on the Throne of Life. It will help restore happiness, hope and unity in our communities and neighbourhoods.

The reason why Mr. Realistic remains so popular is because he's a warrior and gorilla reporter fighting for mental, economical and spiritual freedom and unity and will dare others to enter where other people would not dare enter the places where crime and violence happen every day. It's time to get the message out, "IT'S TIME FOR BLACKS TO STOP KILLING BLACKS". If this continues, we will be like the dinosaur, extinct. No community or neighbourhood can survive by killing or jailing people.

Mr. Realistic's writings are a gift from Creation that he is sharing with truth seekers so that they can feel proud of their homeland, their roots and to never forget the only way We the People are going to see change and reform is when everyone returns to having manners, respect, love and good intentions for one another in their heart and mind. Joining the Creator's original plan and following the Laws of Creation will be another way for people to see change and reform take place in our communities and neighbourhoods that are now lacking guidance.

It's time to prevent the breach of peace and freedom our ancestors fought and died for 500 years ago. Returning to having manners, respect, love and good intentions for one another must become the lightening rod of lasting change and reform in our communities and neighbourhoods. The time has come for no more excuses and it's time to KEEP IT REAL. That's why Mr. Realistic is so popular now. In the 21st century, he keeps it real all the time.

No more IOU's when it comes to telling the truth to the people who are suffering or being oppressed on a daily basis. It's time non truth seekers stop running after money, material things and start praising the Creator and following the Laws of Creation to the fullest every day. Always remember the Creator's original plan is the mind and having manners, love, respect and good intentions for one another is the body of Creation. The time has come for these positive feelings, attitudes and actions to come as naturally and normally to young people and children as crying comes to a baby. They are not something that can be faked. You either have it or you don't have it.

Mr. Realistic's objective is to give truth seekers the best writing he can manufacture in the pursuit of the perfection of having manners, love, respect and good intentions for one another. No matter what he writes, it's always identifiable with the in crown of truth seekers. His interpretation of the simplicity and primitive force of old time spirituals that are a thing of the past like, We Shall Overcome or Ain't Gonne Let Nobody Turn Me Around. It's time to listen, read and enjoy the most refreshing writer to come along in quite some time to lead non-truth seekers back to having manners, respect, love and good intentions.

No college graduation or degree is needed. The only thing that is needed is an open mind and a clean heart. Remarkable writing quality and ability is only one of the exceptional attributes possessed by Mr. Realistic because he pours his soul, heart and the truth into all of his writings. That's why they are so impressive to real truth seekers and his popularity will continue to increase for many more years to come. Genuine talent will always rise to the top with truth seekers and such is the case with Mr. Realistic.

It's time to truly embrace his popularity. It's nothing fake, it's always REEL.
POPULARITY

ALL RIGHTS RESERVED
11-20-2011

KEEPING IT REAL V MYTH

By
Mr. Dave R. Queeley

Keeping It Real is now a real true MYTH.

All my peoples are real respectable people especially you, Samuel Blyden. Keeping It Real is continuing to attack the counterfeiters in the 21st century. Fake thugs can't continue to drift from reality. Keeping It Real does not have the luxury of time to wait on fake thugs to start acting, living and working to promote and support the Creator's original plan and following the Laws of Creation as an everyday activity. This message of Keeping It Real is fire. It's time to expose the MYTHS.

Fake thugs have the misconceptions that evil will be victorious over good in the future. If this ever happens, it will be an epic mental and spiritual disaster that cannot be averted because it will cripple the entire world. In the 21st century it seems that life will continue to regress back to the mental and spiritual dark ages of the cave man. Fake thugs have to overstand that it's never too late for them to take on a new pioneering role of reviving having manners, respect, love and good intentions for one another back into our communities and neighbourhoods as an everyday activity.

We the People continue to struggle to find the answer to the single most important question that needs to be answered, where has the respect, love and good intentions for one another gone? The time has come for these positive feelings, attitudes and actions to spread rapidly throughout our communities, neighbourhoods and maybe the world once and for all so that all the evil wars overseas and at home will finally come to an end. Then injustice and darkness aka planned doom will finally be buried without any resurrection happening in the future. We the People cannot continue to avoid all the noise that the offsprings of injustice and darkness which are "greed is good" and hatred continue making in our communities and neighbourhoods without taking some sort of positive action to stop this noise.

Only we can make sure that this happens and the MYTH of Keeping It Reel does not continue to grow. This MYTH continues to affect our communities and neighbourhoods on an alarming rate without any end, TKO and solution in sight. The re-establishment of Keeping It Real is never on fake thug's itinerary of life. These evil types of people will never be involved in the restoration of having manners, respect, love and good intention for one another, because it makes no money, the root of all evil. Fake thugs have to overstand that these positive feelings, attitudes and actions are the first and most important steps to Keeping It Real. Fake thugs are always the negative misrepresentation of Good over evil at all times.

In the 21st century they are now full of deceit and are surrounded by a whole lot of negativity, disrespect, dishonor and disunity every single day that goes by. They keep on forgetting that Good over evil is the new mental and spiritual battle field and the only weapon that is needed to retaliate is manners, respect, love and good intentions for one another, never any of those manmade evil gadgets of SELF destruction and death aka the gun. These people have to overstand that on the battlefield of Good over evil at all times there is no copyright infringement on Keeping It Real, manners, respect, love and good intentions for one another. They are free to be used all day, every day as the antenna of injustice and darkness is always up putting out evil and negative signals that has some people mentally and spiritually confused about life on the battlefield of Good over evil at all times.

They remain injustice and darkness mercenaries who will commit the greatest sin of Creation, which is take someone's' life. It's now like climate change; it needs attention ASAP because the evidence is clear and adding up every single day that goes by. We the People have no real true strategy, plan and solution to stop our communities and neighbourhoods from being hit by the tidal wave of injustice and darkness that will push them to the brink of physical extinction. Manners, respect, love and good intentions for one another have not gained worldwide attention in our communities and neighbourhoods. This is one of the main reasons why the MYTH of Keeping It Real continues to stay alive in our communities and neighbourhoods without any end in sight.

Fake thugs have to overstand that serving and seeking injustice and darkness is like falling under the ice of a frozen pond for hours. They have no pulse when they are pulled out but could be revived just like having manners, respect, love and good intentions for one another needs to be revived in our communities and neighbourhoods. When mental and spiritual hypothermia sets in, all bets are off. They are dead. Injustice and darkness' power will start to decline sharply. When faith in the Supreme Being's original plan and following the Laws of Creation begins to rise to superstar status. When this happens, having manners, respect, love and good intentions for one another will once again become a highlight reel every single day that goes by that can be played on Sports Center's Top 10 on ESPN.

Our communities and neighbourhoods have disintegrated into a lawless cesspool and swamp of fake thuggery (gangs), gun violence, racism, hard drugs and crime. It's time to pull the plug on injustice and darkness because We the People are being swamped by the undigested evil and negative feelings. Attitudes and actions of "greed is good" and hatred on a regular basis. This makes it seem like it's impossible to delete the MYTH of Keeping It Real from the people, young and old mind, body and soul who remain in mental and spiritual captivity. Fake thugs would rather trade their mind, body and soul for being rich and famous people who would go on to carry this evil and negative success like it's a beautiful championship trophy.

In the 21st century the MYTH of Keeping It Real has hundreds of fake thugs still dying trying to reach their mental and spiritual peak of life which is SELF LOVE. The real true statement and example of Good over evil at all times in our image conscious world. The MYTH of Keeping It Real is a powerful message of when you get in trouble with the law, do not9 become a CI; wear a wire and start snitching so that they can get their time cut short. We have to stand together in condemning this deadly and dangerous MYTH once and for all.

It does more harm than good. BELIEVE IT OR NOT.

ALL RIGHTS RESERVED
05-07-2014

DEAR CARNIVAL
By
Mr. Dave R. Queeley

Dear Carnival,

Before the Ourstory Recorder aka V.I. Hit Factory gets started, he wants to give the people, young and old a short history lesson about how Carnival got started. Carnival got its start as the story goes; in 1911 Virgin Islander Adolph "Ding" Sixto attended a Carnival in Rio de Janeiro, Brazil. He was so awed by that experience that Mt. Sixto brought the concept back home to the Virgin Islands. On February 14, 1912, while the islands were still under Danish rule, the first St. Thomas Carnival was held.

This successful event was repeated until the advent of World War I, when it came to a halt. When in 1952 a St. Thomas radio announcer by the name of Ron DeLugo heard Puerto Rico was planning to host a Carnival event. Inspired by the idea, he announced to the listening public, that if Puerto Rico could host such an affair, St. Thomas has the ability to do it even better. So they did. In 2015, it will be making 63 years young. So thank you Ron DeLugo, the first Delegate from the US Virgin Islands appointed to the US House of Representatives for the annual party we now call CARNIVAL.

2013 was an embarrassment to everyone who took part in Jou'vert, but 2014 was not. It was real true mass; whole place wet with paint and powdered down. 2014 Jou'vert started off on the right foot at 4:01 am with a steel band playing muzik up and down the road. I cannot remember the name of the steel band, but nuff respect for a job well done. Jou'vert arriving at the Carnival finishing line alive and in one piece was a blessing to all who came out in 2014. It was really the biggest fete ever seen.

Once again thank you to all the evil doers, bad man and fake thugs who stayed home or who took the Ourstory Recorder's advice to leave the gun at home and come out and bust a whine. The more light We the People shine on Jou'vert about the disrespect of our ancestors past story the safer it will become in the future otherwise it will become an endangered species just like the white tiger. The only black eye to 2014 Jou'vert was that damn helicopter circling above making all that noise, but if that is what it takes for Jou'vert to reach the Carnival finishing line. We the People can deal with it.

We the People have to overstand that in 2014 we have made the courageous decisions to party without any B. S. violence happening that would have caused V. I. P. D. to pull the plug on Jou'vert. 2014 Jou'vert wants to say thank you to all those trouble makers for holding it down. Duty tradition from dying of a slow death. It's time to take things to a whole new level of having respect, love and good intentions for one another. 2014 Jou'vert was more evidence we should stick with and save our culture, heritage and tradition.

They were passed down from our ancestors. It's our job, and responsibility to keep them alive as we move forward deeper into the century of the unknown. It's no secret everyone needs to learn about and have S. W. A. G., which now means Start Working Against Gun violence and crime. So 2015 Jou'vert can also go down in Carnival history as another safe and joyous One Love tramp up the road.

The Ourstory Recorder wants to say thank you and nuff respect to all the bands who took part in 2014 Jou'vert. He wants to give a special shout out to Cool Session and Triple K bands. The Ourstory Recorder wants to tell the world that he endorses the D. A. Printers all day, every day. Seeing is believing, not hearing.

Once again, nuff respect and let's keep it moving; Carnival wants to say THANK YOU for not spoiling the party with shots being fired. THANK YOU very much for your time, We the People love you Jou'vert and will do anything to keep you alive.

THANKS FOR LISTENING CARNIVAL!

IT WAS REALLY THE BIGGEST FETE EVER SEEN: CARNIVAL 2014

ALL RIGHTS RESERVED
05-06-2014

Read on The Avalanche Radio Show on 05/06/2014

OUR DUTY AND JOB
By
Mr. Dave R. Queeley

NO MORE TOXIC RELATIONSHIP

In the 21st century, it's every Mahogany man's JOB AND DUTY in life to make sure the Mahogany woman always feels like a QUEEN everyday that goes by, her beauty comes in many different shades. So it's time to have respect, love and good intentions for one another on a daily basis for the Creator's greatest gift to man, which is the woman and not the gun, it's man-made. All Mahogany men have to understand and realize that respect, love and good intentions for one another will make sure monogamy is exciting once again until DEATH DO US PART.

Monogamy is everlasting if it's always involved with respect, love and good intentions for one another. The disrespect, inequality and hatred Mahogany people face around the world is still hard to believe going deeper into the 21st century; that's why monogamy is so important to continue climbing up the mountain of respect, love and good intentions for one another until we reach the top and the Creator's original plan and Laws of Creation is the highest and top priority in life. Only then respect, love and good intentions for one another will start coming out and blooming like a flower on a tree.

In the 21st century everything a Mahogany woman needs in her life is right at her finger tips and some of these women continue to refuse to use them. They are SELF RESPECT, SELF CONTROL, SELF CONFIDENCE, SELF LOVE and most of all SELF PRIDE. All these feelings, attitudes and actions will make sure in the 21st century they start respecting and treating one another better. These feelings, attitudes and actions will not leave them feeling frustrated and unimpressed by "Good over Evil" at no point in life. These feelings, attitudes and actions have long been ignored by some of them for a while. They keep on forgetting that "Good over Evil" goes way beyond their physical beauty, tight clothes and the prostitute mentality that many of them have been living with for years.

Fighting for respect, love and good intentions for one another should be their way of life; because back in the good old days of living and working in the Motherland aka Africa, when Mahogany women were QUEENS, they use to control the power of culture and built the awareness of the family within the Creator's original plan, especially how to follow the Laws of Creation without making any mistakes, ensuring their family members stay on the right pathway of "Good over Evil" at all times.

In the 21st century these feelings, attitudes and actions are now a lost art form to so Mahogany women because they remain mentally and spiritually dead, believing that "greed is good" when it's not good at all. It only leads to SELF destruction and death. These women keep on forgetting that real true beauty is all about these feelings, attitudes and actions being a part of their lives on a day to day basis without any end in sight. In the 21st century it seems that some Mahogany women have lost appreciation for their past as QUEENS and have settled for being called "whore" and "bitch" by their life partner. They keep on forgetting, without their past they will not be able to map out a real true game plan of being mentally and spiritually successful in the future.

Mahogany women have to have a zero tolerance policy when it comes to being called by these evil names. They have to start demanding that the Mahogany man get on his JOB AND DUTY and start respecting and treating her like the QUEEN she is and start dismantling all negative and evil mentality towards this QUEEN once and for all; because a house without a woman and man is an empty house that is full of injustice and darkness aka planned doom. When the Mahogany man starts getting on his JOB AND DUTY; respect, love and good intentions for one another will energize their minds, bodies and souls to do what's right and positive in life to make sure the Mahogany woman always feels like a QUEEN, no matter what happens in life, good or bad.

If Mahogany women and men start living and working together as a family unit, it's no telling how high and far we will rise in the battle of "Good over Evil". We have to understand that having respect, love and good intention for one another are the greatest gifts anyone can give the Creator on a daily basis. In the 21st century Mahogany men have to be bold, courageous and put the Mahogany woman second in life after the Creator. It's the only way to be mentally and spiritually successful living and working in the New World of injustice and darkness aka planned doom. It's now a place where mental and spiritual Utopia does not exist, but respect, love and good intentions for one another shines through darkness all day, every day without any end in sight.

Mahogany men have to realize "greed is good" and hatred is an artificial mental and spiritual block for them to do what's right, good and positive to make sure the Mahogany woman always knows she is always qualified and never an embarrassment to being called a QUEEN. The time has come for no more mental and spiritual diversions. It's time Mahogany men get on their JOB AND DUTY and live their lives to the fullest and be a real true inspiration to the next generation of Mahogany women like a QUEEN once again.

When this starts happening, the sky will be the limit to respect, love and good intentions for one another that she will receive from her KING. Our DUTY AND JOB is a direct message to all Mahogany men that they have to always remember the Mahogany woman is not GOD, but she is the next best thing or the closest anyone can feel to GOD

So all Mahogany men you better recognize, it's our DUTY AND JOB to treat, respect and make sure she always feels like SHE'S MY QUEEN.

ALL RIGHTS RESERVED
12-06-2014

ARE YOU A BAD MAN
By
Mr. Dave R. Queeley

If you're a BAD MAN on the streets of injustice and darkness aka planned doom, you have to be badder in jail or prison; you have to become more dangerous and deadly than you were on the streets. There is no running away and no crying, its fight to the death for respect; otherwise your manhood will be disrespected. In jail or prison there is no punk peace, it's only unity with colour bangers or death if you're a BAD MAN on the streets.

The Ourstory Recorder wants all fake thugs to know there are no good stories about going to the pit of mental and spiritual doom; its worst than taking heroin, cocaine and ecstasy all together at one time. As a citizen the Ourstory Recorder have a lot of concerns as to why fake ass thugs keep on acting like they are BAD MEN. If you feel like a BAD MAN keep it to yourself. We the People are sick and tired of all those fake ass thugs causing all those senseless, random and unnecessary shootings and killings that keep on happening in our communities and neighbourhoods on a daily basis.

If you really want to be a BAD MAN join the army and then you can kill as much people as you want and get paid for it. Now that's a real BAD MAN in the Ourstory Recorder's eye sight. Sometimes the Ourstory Recorder wonders what happened to BAD MAN, why they don't want to look into the crystal ball of truth and honour to sight up the Creator, the Almighty who protects We the People on the battle field and pathways of evil and disaster; If we all become real truth seekers and not just in words aka lip service but in deeds.

Truth and honour which are special feelings still deep within all the people who remain in mental and spiritual captivity, acting like BAD MEN. They keep on forgetting that these feelings are always ready to burst out and help good to be victorious in the battle for world supremacy against evil at all times. Fake thugs keep on forgetting real BAD MEN talk the truth and think twice about anything they do in life, and they trust and respect one another, because they know their life's duty is to make sure Good over Evil happens at all points in life.

Non truth seekers and evil doers aka BAD MAN have to always remember the curtains of hopelessness, greed, disrespect, dishonour and disunity is finally closing because We the People will continue putting more and more of the mental and spiritual pieces that are needed in life together to make sure the evil mentality of being a BAD MAN dies once and for all in our communities and neighbourhoods. This will ensure that Good over Evil can be successful as we move forward deeper and deeper into the 21st century having manners, respect, love and good intentions for one another as the new mentality that We the People are now trying very hard to create within our communities and neighbourhoods so that extinction does not happen in the future.

Knowing the truth should be everyone's business, not "Greed is good and hatred" anymore. These feelings, attitudes and actions keep the enemies alive in our communities and neighbourhoods, which are hopelessness, greed, disrespect, dishonour and disunity which only leads to SELF destruction and death, maybe extinction happening in the future of Good over Evil. Fake thugs aka BAD MAN have to understand that manners, respect, love and good intentions for one another are not a luxury reserved for the privileged few, but it's the animating force behind Good over Evil at all times.

When having manners, respect, love and good intentions for one another are practiced every day, it will be seen as a symbol of mental and spiritual restorations of our communities and neighbourhoods where the BAD MAN mentality will not exist anymore. These feelings, attitudes and actions have to be practiced like a new dance move. We the People have to always remember fake thugs aka BAD MAN will never surrender their minds, bodies and souls to anything that is positive and good in life. These feelings, attitudes and actions will never lead to non truth seekers and evil doers aka BAD MAN being victorious in the battle of Good over Evil at no point in life.

If these feelings, attitudes and actions continue to happen it will lead to total destruction and maybe extinction of the people who are Mahogany, because BLACK ON BLACK crime is not a positive signal to Good over Evil ever happening in this lifetime. In the 21st century fake thugs are not the curator of manners, respect, love and good intentions for one another anymore. Evil doers and non truth seekers aka BAD MAN have to finally understand that staying true to oneself and focusing on Good over Evil are the real true rules of life to live by if they want to be mentally and spiritually successful in the future, in the battle of Good over Evil.

Their vision for having manners, respect, love and good intentions for one another are not boundless. So they are not inspired to do good and positive things in life. They are not visionaries but are A**holes in life. WHY?

SO...

ARE YOU A BAD MAN?

TELL ME WHY.

01/05/2014
ALL RIGHTS RESERVED
Read on The Avalanche Radio Show on 01/22/2014

CHANGE OUR BEHAVIOR
By
Mr. Dave R. Queeley

Thank you Jade Rawlins for this name on 01-06-2014.

WE AREN'T ANIMALS!

Black on Black crime should be the justification that is needed for We the People to make the critical mental and spiritual changes that would help stop all those senseless random and unnecessary shootings and killings that continue to happen in our communities and neighborhoods with no end in sight for miles. In the 21st century, it seems We the People will never be committed to undertaking the changes that are necessary to ensure that Good over Evil is the people's, young and old, motto of life as we move forward, deeper and deeper into the 21st Century of the unknown. It's time to stop talking about BLACK ON BLACK crime and start acting and working to stop it now before reality sets in, which is extinction.

BLACK ON BLACK crime keeps our communities and neighborhoods mentally and spiritually incompetent and divided. So it's time We the People start supporting and promoting the Creator's original plan and Laws of Creation as our top and highest priority. BLACK ON BLACK crime only happens because greed is good and hatred is always on some people's minds and in their bodies and souls who can now be called non truth seekers aka evil doers. These people keep on forgetting that greed is good and hatred will never help them get to the core of Good over Evil at no point in life. Respect, love and good intentions for one another will automatically give anyone who is involved with it, the vision to find new ways to make sure Good over Evil is fulfilled like prophecy.

BLACK ON BLACK crime leaves some people disbelieving that manners, respect, love and good intentions will never ever return to our communities and neighborhoods as an everyday activity that is practiced by We the People without any more time outs and blackouts happening. BLACK ON BLACK crime, greed is good and hatred has caused lingering doubts about when this return will ever happen in our communities and neighborhoods. CHANGE IS GOOD, so if We the People CHANGE OUR BEHAVIOR and stop being afraid of mental and spiritual change and start supporting the Creator's original plan and make sure the Laws of Creation are followed on a day to day basis, we can finally see a real true end to BLACK ON BLACK crime. Our communities and neighborhoods will then once again become a safe place to live, work and visit at anytime night or day; it will be safe.

Only then We the People will start to see a real true decline in all those senseless, random, and unnecessary shootings and killings that some people think and believe will not come to an end no time soon unless extinction happens. In the 21st century, respect, love and good intentions for one another will make sure the people, young and old are not so easily caught up and entrapped by these evil feelings, attitudes and actions that keeps the deviant behavior to Good over Evil alive in our communities and neighborhoods. We the People need to change having the evil philosophy of greed is good and BLACK ON BLACK crime because it's mentally and spiritually exhausting and does more harm than anyone can imagine to Good over Evil being successful in our communities and neighborhoods in the future. We have to CHANGE OUR BEHAVIOR so that these evil and negative lifestyle and mentality can start declining on a daily basis until the prophecy of Good over Evil is fulfilled.

We have to always remember no one is exempt from the mental and spiritual hardships of life while on the journey of Good over Evil at all times so they never lose faith in this monumental victory that will soon happen which is good will finally defeat evil in the battle for world supremacy. In the 21st century, some people have no pride, tradition and passion for Good over Evil so they remain mentally and spiritually dead, who continue to be involved with BLACK ON BLACK crime, greed is good and hatred as their highest and top priority in life. These evil and negative feelings, attitudes and actions are now trying to pummel We the People into mental and spiritual submission in the 21st century

It's time to CHANGE OUR BEHAVIOR because extinction is forever believe it or not.

CLONING WILL NOT WORK!

ALL RIGHTS RESERVED
12/07/2013
Read on The Avalanche Radio Show on 01/09/2014

PARADISE GONE
By
Mr. Dave R. Queeley

Pay-to-Play and Live

The myth of the classless society has to be exposed!

Welcome to the Pay-to-Play and Live paradise, where if you have money to grease the wheels of injustice and darkness aka planned doom, you can do whatever you want, even get away with first degree murder. Lack of accountability in Joe Bogus aka the Government is the core problem and reason why life in America's so called Paradise is going down the drain fast; like a runaway freight train. Some people continue to maintain the myth that Paradise is in no clear and present danger of going bankrupt and Paradise is running good.

The time has come for We the People to come to grips with this evil situation and find real true solutions before it's too damn late for any type of action to work. We the People must always remember, back in the days of peace, freedom and unity there was nothing artificial, negative, corrupt and dangerous about life in America's so called Paradise. Everyone had manners, respect, love and good intentions for one another on their minds and in their bodies and souls before greed is good and hatred, bad policies and bad Government invaded the realm of life in paradise, causing the people in charge, who are policy makers, to have a limited vision of doing what's right and positive for the people who are suffering and being oppressed on a daily basis in America's so called Paradise.

They now need a how to manual on how to operate as men and women of honour and respect. They continue resisting the essential reforms and changes that are needed to improving their failing government system. It sometimes feels like they have no intention of figuring out how to best address the social ills that has life in America's so called Paradise going down the drain faster than a speeding bullet. There are a lot of allegations of Pay-to-Play and Live going on in America's so called Paradise. We the People now have hard evidence that our so called policy makers aka MODERN DAY PIRATES, has been involved in several cases of Pay-to-Play and Live deals and first degree robberies over the last couple of decades.

The time has come for these Pay-to-Play and Live deals and robberies to stop and any policy makers aka MODERN DAY PIRATES who are involved with these deals and cases should receive a 25 year sentence when they are found guilty, with no parole. This will be the first real true step in telling these educated criminals, We the People are not going to continue to tolerate these feelings, attitudes and actions anymore. We must never forget about the Pay-to-Play and Live deals with Captain Morgan Rum and the

6.9 million dollar robbery without a gun should not slip or fade away from our minds. We the People must never forget no one has ever been named or charged for these backroom deals and crimes against humanity.

Some people have now alleged that the policy makers aka MODERN DAY PIRATES working in the executive branch might have taken a cut of the stolen loot. The executive power and privileges are the ones that are always subject to abuse their power. If these educated criminals continue to hold this office, whose mind, body and soul are blinded by greed is good and hatred, disrespect, dishonour, and disunity while the people continue suffering and being oppressed on a daily basis with no end in sight. It seems to some people in the 21st century that the people who are policy makers aka MODERN DAY PIRATES are planning and trying to make a paradise just for the privileged few who have the money to grease the wheels of injustice and darkness aka planned doom. They are always willing and ready to Pay-to-Play and Live in America's so called Paradise.

We the People have to become the main agents for political, economic, social change and reform in America's so called Paradise because the people who are working for Joe Bogus aka the Government have no vision, action or plan to decolonization and development of America's so called Paradise. They are very happy to steer sweetheart deals to their friends and allies. In the 21st century there are thousands of people that now disapprove of the way both

Republicans and Democrats are doing their job in the executive, legislative and supreme branches. This makes them look like a bunch of a...holes and fools in the public and world eyes.

Lately there has been an evil tendency on the part of our BS administration to try and hide behind their executive, supreme and legislative privilege and power every time there is something shady taking place in this government system. The people who are policy makers aka MODERN DAY PIRATES that have their definition of working for the people which is doing nothing and waiting for problems to solve themselves which can never happen without work. These evil people keep on forgetting our electric company is so badly managed that small businesses are being decimated every month because they can't pay their high ass electricity bill and this does more harm than good to America's so called Paradise economy.

America's so called Paradise has been plagued by decades of corruption and mismanagement. The people who are policy makers aka MODERN DAY PIRATES have engaged in an evil pattern of discriminatory and unconstitutional activity that can now be called a state of emergency. Some people see politics in America's so called Paradise as a spectator sport or a popularity contest. It's time for We the People to get out of the stands of injustice and darkness cheering and get down on the playing field or court of having manners, respect, love and good intentions for one another and start trying to find real true solutions to all the social ills and problems We the People face on a regular basis.

Political in house fighting has put heavy limitations on Joe Bogus aka the Government doing what's right or being positive examples for all to see. Our Government system is now, so weak enough that it needs an IV to stay alive. Right now it needs true cooperation of all forces that are involved with manners, respect, love and good intentions for one another; only then more and more people will be getting angry, because of the very poor public service that is being provided to the people who are suffering and being oppressed on a daily basis in America's so called Paradise.

Security at our borders are absent, that's why there is so many guns and drugs on the streets running rampantly on a daily basis. In the 21st century, We the People are not demanding better treatment and conditions. The removal of all and evil and the BS administration as soon as possible is needed so that the evil and negative mentality that America's so called Paradise is up for sale at all times can stop.

NO MORE PAY-TO-PLAY AND LIVE.

IT'S NOT WORTH IT AT ALL!

ALL RIGHTS RESERVED
01/11/2014

NOTHING
By
Mr. Dave R. Queeley

In the 21st century NOTHING seems to be working very well to stop fake thuggery (gangs), gun violence and crime from moving forward and staying alive in our communities and neighborhoods. We the People now need a grassroots mental and spiritual activism, compelling the people, young and old to take a more forceful stand against these evil feelings, attitudes and actions that will only lead to SELF destruction, death and maybe extinction in the future. In the 21st century, some people are still saying, believing and thinking that hatred is still the most important issue We the People face especially if they are a Mahogany Man living and working in our communities and neighborhoods.

The time has come to spread the GOOD NEWS aka the Word, among Mahogany People especially young people and children that their skin color, culture and heritage should always be a real true source of pride and not a source of hatred, dishonor, disrespect, disunity and hopelessness. This source of pride will make sure they stop feeling worthless, unwanted and not good for nothing that is good in life. Well, THAT'S A LIE. Words have real true power to change some things in life.

We the People have to remember the threat of extinction remains very real. We have to remember respect, love and good intentions for one another is a social obligation of all people, young and old who are anointed with the mentality of Good over Evil and knows it's their duty and job to help stop fake ass thuggery, gun violence and crime from moving forward and staying alive in our communities and neighborhoods causing mental and spiritual tension and havoc on a daily basis with no real true end in sight. Respect, love and good intentions for one another will pierce through the evil elements of injustice and darkness aka planned doom with velocity and the tightness of the spiral of a football.

All the people living and working in our communities and neighborhoods have to always remember everything that is good in life requires hard work and it's a good lesson for all young people and children to learn about going deeper and deeper into the 21st century. This will help them to avoid senseless, random and unnecessary dangers in life, because nothing can stop you from being successful in the future, but YOURSELF. Always remember that life is not a game and it's too damn short. Our communities and neighborhoods has a reputation as an evil and lawless place to live, work and visit because of a scant police presence in our communities and neighborhoods that has now turned into a place where mental and spiritual executions happen on a daily basis.

In the 21st century, some people are saying, thinking and believing that the only way to stop fake thuggery, gun violence and crime is with a police precinct in every community and neighborhood with officers patrolling 24 hours, 7 days a week without any more BS-ing around. We do not need those police officers who are too quick to reach for their weapons of destruction and death. These weapons are their flashlights, batons and sometimes their guns. We need police officers who will work hand in hand with the people living and working in our communities and neighborhoods to make sure we see a decline in all those senseless, random and unnecessary shootings and killings. We the People keep on forgetting our communities and neighborhoods set per capita homicide rate in 2010, where the rate hit more than 60 homicides per 100,000 residents.

We need a real true mental and spiritual approach to de-escalating all those random, senseless and unnecessary shootings and killings that is now a real every day problem we continue to face, especially if you're a Mahogany Man. Death is always around the corner if you're involved with fake thuggery, gun violence and crime on a regular basis. We have to remember the growth of having respect, love and good intentions for one another has started to slow down all around the world. These feelings, attitudes and actions use to be the back bone of our communities and neighborhoods before some people allowed greed is good and hatred to take over their lives and has kept them living and working in the lion's den of hopelessness, greed, disrespect, dishonor and disunity on a daily basis with no end in sight.

If these evil feelings, attitudes and actions continue, extinction will be upon us very soon. We the People now have the perfect opportunity to alleviate these evil feelings, attitudes and actions out of our communities and neighborhoods by starting to spread the Creator's original plan and Laws of Creation all across the world as an everyday activity. It's time to say. ..

GOOD RIDDANCE TO DOING NOTHING

ALL RIGHTS RESERVED
11-12-2013

USE TO BE GRIMY
By
Mr. Dave R. Queeley

The Ourstory Recorder aka the V.I. Hit Factory use to live on the grimy side of life and knows that without manners, respect, love and good intentions for one another. We the People will continue to be like a tree without any roots, it cannot live or survive another 500 years. Without these positive feelings, attitudes and actions the people will continue to promote and support "greed is good" at all times, hatred and war on a daily basis. "Greed is good", hatred and war are never the keys of life to being successful in the battle of Good over Evil.

The Ourstory Recorder knows living grimy; the enemies are hopelessness, greed, disrespect, dishonour and disunity which are mental and spiritual obstacles to happiness and joy being a part of anyone's life. Without manners, respect, love and good intentions for one another We the People will never have any mental and spiritual gravity, just free falling head first into the evil pit of eternal hellfire.

The Ourstory Recorder knows the privileged few wants to lock up all the righteous truth seekers and throw away the key because they are trouble makers who are always on the streets promoting and supporting the Creator's original plan and Laws of Creation as an everyday activity that will lead to everyone being victorious in the battle of Good over Evil.

The Ourstory Recorder is the new poster child for mental and spiritual reform and change that is long overdue in some people's lives. In the 21st century the Ourstory Recorder knows there are three types of people living and working in our communities and neighbourhoods, The ones who approve of manners, respect, love and good intentions being an everyday activity; the ones who are doing nothing and disapprove of these positive feelings, attitudes and actions as an everyday activity; And the ones who are just haters of anything that has to do with Good over Evil at all times , especially if they own one of those evil man made gadgets of SELF destruction and death aka the GUN.

They keep on forgetting that owning a GUN is an enormous mental and spiritual conflict of interest that does not enhance manners, respect, love and good intentions for one another at no point in life. There is no award or reward for having manners, respect, love and good intentions for one another as a top and highest priority in life. This is one of the main reasons why it's on the decline in our communities and neighbourhoods on a daily basis. These positive feelings, attitudes and actions are the principles of granting and maintaining the special and divine rights of Good over Evil at all times.

This message of USE TO BE GRIMY is to let the people, young and old know it's never too late to start rebuilding their mental and spiritual lives day by day. If they are involved with having manners, respect, love and good intentions on a daily basis, only then rebuilding their mental and spiritual lives will become easier to accomplish in the future. When this happens, the people, young and old will become real true crusaders for the Creator's original plan which is, "Good will conquer Evil and Love will triumph over Hate" and follow the Laws of Creation without breaking any of them.

It will always be on their minds and in their bodies and souls while on the battle field of Good over Evil. These feelings, attitudes and actions will make sure the people, young and old stop living on the grimy side of life where the enemies of respect, love and good intentions are the Messiah. These enemies are always hopelessness, greed, disrespect, dishonour, and disunity which are always a part of this evil conglomerate of injustice and darkness aka planned doom.

No more window shopping when it comes to having manners, respect, love and good intentions for one another is a real true effort to resolving the mounting mental and spiritual tension between the people that is reflected in the way we communicate and treat one another on a daily basis. We the People have to make sure that Good is victorious against Evil in the final battle for world supremacy. We the People have to know exactly what we want to do in life, good or bad; and figure out how we are going to get it done, ASAP.

We have a considerable way to go to be mentally and spiritually successful in the battle of Good over Evil in the future. Having manners, respect, love and good intentions for one another will stop the people young and old from continuing to sink deeper and deeper into the evil waters of injustice and darkness aka planned doom once and for all as we move forward deeper and deeper into the century of the unknown. These people who are sinking into the evil waters of injustice and darkness has no mental and spiritual integrity and has no personal connection and sense of loyalty to show that having manners, respect, love and good intentions for one another are still a valued part of the team of Good over Evil.

They keep on forgetting that these positive feelings, attitudes and actions have to be compared just like singing a church hymn on Sundays from the top of the lungs. In the 21st century some people are horrified that manners, respect, love and good intentions for one another have been discredited by the people, young and old, who live within some parts of our communities and neighbourhoods that has fallen under the strict laws and rules of injustice and darkness aka planned doom. This has poured more gasoline on the raging mental and spiritual wildfires and conflicts that are feeding on one another and complicating the already complex mental and spiritual struggle of Good over Evil so that it does not take firmer roots in our communities, neighbourhoods and world.

The Ourstory Recorder is on the streets of injustice and darkness aka planned doom recording the reality that some people are afraid to talk about out loud in the public because they fear losing their jobs, but no one can fire the Ourstory Recorder. The Creator got him hired to always tell it like it is without any sugar coating; because living on the grimy side of life having manners, respect, love and good intentions for one another will never be like a rainbow coming out after the rain has gone away to come back another day.

Living grimy is just an illusion that keeps some people from promoting and supporting Good over Evil at all times.

STOP BEING GRIMY!!

HAPPY BIRTHDAY BROTHER, A. QUEELEY

ALL RIGHTS RESERVED
01/11/2014

NO EXPIRATION DATE
By
Mr. Dave R. Queeley

In the 21st century some Mahogany men think and believe that loving, respecting and having good intentions for the Mahogany woman is the worst experience they can have in their lives. These foolish men keep on forgetting that the worst experience of life is owning one of those evil man made gadgets of SELF destruction and death aka the GUN and pulling the trigger and taking someone's life for no good and godly reason under the sun, moon and stars. All Mahogany men have to remember loving, respecting and having good intentions for the Mahogany woman has NO EXPIRATION DATE on it. It's supposed to last a lifetime when it comes to the Creator's greatest creation and gift to man, THE WOMAN.

These men have to remember a race of people that do not educate about Good over Evil and keep their families safe, is a race of men who will lose their women to the enemies and will not be around much longer. The reestablishment of having manners, respect, love and good intentions for the Mahogany woman should always be the top and highest priority on Mahogany men's itinerary on a regular basis as they move forward deeper and deeper into the century of the unknown. These positive feelings, attitudes and actions should always be first on the Mahogany man's mind and in their bodies and souls when they awake in the morning after Giving Thanks to the Creator for life.

There should be no mental and spiritual obstacles that should prevent the Mahogany man from going through thick and thin to make sure the Mahogany woman always feels like a QUEEN on a daily basis. Both Mahogany men and women have to fully trust and respect each other to make the best decisions in life, doing it with best of intentions and not selfish intentions. They must realize that change, whether good or bad always comes. By having a real true life's partner by your side somehow makes the challenges life throws at you a little less scary and a lot more empowering for Good to be victorious over Evil at all times.

The Mahogany men who are not involved with supporting and promoting loving, respecting and having good intentions for the Mahogany woman, needs to be declared mentally and spiritually sick and unfit and will face the real true consequences of dying lonely. Promoting and supporting these positive feelings, attitudes and actions should be like an Arctic blast that will freeze up the world of injustice and darkness aka planned doom. It's a Mahogany man's duty and job to seek and find new ways to achieve a higher standard of living for the Mahogany woman who has already been affected by the seeds of prejudice and hatred.

A real Mahogany man knows it's virtually impossible to stop loving, respecting and having good intentions for the Mahogany woman, the first BEAUTY QUEEN of Creation. Respect, love and good intentions will make sure the Mahogany man finds their inner sixth sense because it's a strong intuition with the great mental and spiritual abilities to do what's right and positive in life for the Mahogany woman to be mentally and spiritually successful in the future of Good over Evil. Mahogany men have to stop publicly humiliating the Mahogany woman in the 21st century by continuously forgetting that the Anglo-Saxon woman is the Mahogany man's mental and spiritual Kryptonite.

YES, the Ourstory Recorder said it. So who FEELS IT, KNOWS IT. Mahogany men have to report for their duties and jobs of generating mental and spiritual growth and loyalty to the first BEAUTY QUEEN of Creation. The time has come to put the Mahogany woman back on the pedestal of Good over Evil and never be called by those evil and negative names such as whore, gold digger, and bitch. They have to stop dressing so provocatively so those evil names are not used to describe them anymore. Mahogany women have to stop feeling like they are being violated by the Mahogany man while evil continues shooting daggers of SELF destruction and death at them so they do not be victorious in the battle of Good over Evil.

When the Mahogany man understands loving, respecting and having good intentions for the Mahogany woman every day, all day; only then the both of them will stop leading separate lives and find real true ways to stay united for another 500 years loving, respecting and having good intentions for one another. The Mahogany woman is the greatest honour and badge that any Mahogany man can have and wear in their life. The Mahogany men who are not involved with these positive feelings, attitudes and actions are several hundred miles away from reality and cannot get slavery out of their minds, bodies and souls and will never be progressive about loving, respecting and having good intentions for the Mahogany woman on a day to day basis with no end or time outs in sight.

These positive feelings, attitudes and actions continue driving an evil wedge between men and women to make positive and good choices for one another and stop violating the Creator's original plan and the Laws of Creation and start seeking the knowledge of respect, love and good intentions. In the 21st century a real Mahogany man knows respect, love and good intentions are the recipes for the mind-enhancing feelings, attitudes and actions of Good over Evil at all times. These feelings, attitudes, and actions will give them the power to do anything that is positive and right in life that will make sure they put the Mahogany woman back on the pedestal of Good over evil and to always remember there is NO EXPIRATION DATE to loving, respecting and having good intentions for the Creator's greatest creation, THE WOMAN.

Some of these men now need mental and spiritual counselling to help them learn how best to work through their mental and spiritual struggles of life without being controlled by the enemies that are hopelessness, greed, disrespect, dishonour and disunity on a daily basis. These men have forgotten that without respect, love and good intentions for one another they stand in danger of being exterminated from the world in the future. They have to realize that these positive feelings, attitudes and actions brings divine mental and spiritual blessing straight from the Creator which is always unconditional.

The Creator is the ALPHA & OMEGA!
I AM ALPHA, SHE IS OMEGA!
WE ARE CREATION, so there is....
NO EXPIRATION DATE

ALL RIGHTS RESERVED
01/14/2014
Read on The Avalanche Radio Show on 01/23/2014

SUBMISSION
By
Mr. Dave R. Queeley

Obviously there is no message to the rivals of the authority of respect, love and good intentions for one another, these rivals keep on forgetting that the battle between Good and Evil is primarily about the struggle of the mind, body and soul of the people who remain in mental and spiritual captivity and are involved with BLACK ON BLACK CRIME, Greed is good and hatred as an everyday activity. Their motto for life is NO SUBMISSION to respect, love and good intentions for one another at no point in life. In the 21st century anti-fake thuggery, gun violence and crime marches, walks and rallies the need to be held every month or every week to let fake thugs know ENOUGH IS ENOUGH and it's time to put down the evil man made gadgets of SELF destruction and death before it's too late for any action to work.

The people who continue to stay away from these marches, walks and rallies now have the reputation as people who don't give a damn when it comes to protecting and keeping our communities and neighbourhoods safe from fake thuggery, gun violence and crime. The mental, spiritual and cultural gaps have been pried further apart by fake thuggery, gun violence and crime causing more bloodshed on a daily basis. Back in the good old days of peace, freedom and unity the authority of respect, love and good intentions for one another was million times more sacred that BLACK ON BLACK CRIME, Greed is Good and hatred, aka unjust treatment.

Fake thuggery, gun violence and crime will begin to disintegrate in rapid fashion when the authority of respect, love and good intentions for one another regain control of the people lives once and for all. It will become the spirit of revolution and not just a lost cause or a deferred dream where no one will ever be in charge; just Greed is good and hatred, running rampantly with no true end in sight. The authority of respect, love and good intentions for one another will represent the movement for social and economic justice for all.

This movement will be energized by truth and honour. It will have an enormous future across the world without ever being infiltrated by Greed is good, BLACK ON CLACK CRIME and hatred again, because the Creator's original plan and the Laws of Creation will be the top and highest priority in life. This popular choice or misunderstanding and miscommunication would not develop anymore if the authority of respect, love and good intentions for one another is widely distributed throughout our communities and neighbourhoods on a daily basis. We the People must definitely have a deeper appreciation for being able to march, walk and attend these rallies without seeing dogs, police officers and fire trucks trying to stop the people.

In the 21st century, life can be quickly taken away by fake thuggery, gun violence and crime. These feelings, attitudes and actions only lead to SELF destruction, death and maybe extinction happening in the future. When We the People mental and spiritual activities have increased in supporting and promoting the authority of respect, love and good intentions for one another on a day to day basis, only then we will see a big drop in the murder and crime rate that is now off the charts of life. BLACK ON BLACK CRIME, Greed is good and hatred are caused by deeply ingrained SELF sabotaging thoughts of injustice and darkness aka planned doom that some people cannot get rid of out of their lives and keep on submitting their minds, bodies and souls to the enemies which are hopelessness, greed, disrespect, dishonour and disunity.

These people have to always remember Good over Evil is a state of consciousness that's achieved by having the authority of respect, love and good intentions for one another as an everyday activity on the battle field of Good over Evil. SUBMISSION means to yield or surrender oneself to the will or authority of another person's ideas and belief in life. We the People have the opportunity to stop submitting to all these evil feelings, attitudes and actions if we just return to having the authority of respect, love and good intentions for one another as part of our lives, only then we will see a bright, successful and prosperous future, one that the people so deeply deserve which is long overdue.

BLACK ON BLACK CRIME, Greed is good and hatred are symbols of the devastation and desperation what is heaped up on the already deeply mentally and spiritually poor people who cannot find their way out of injustice and darkness aka planned doom. The authority of respect, love and good intentions will keep the people on a level mental and spiritual playing field and will never send Good over Evil into cardiac arrest at no point in life, it will always be Happily Ever After at all times.

BLACK ON BLACK CRIME, Greed is good and hatred has no telepathic frequencies that can tap into the subconscious of the people who are involved with the authority of respect, love and good intentions for one another on a daily basis. The people who are involved with this authority will never need any mental and spiritual shelter from the everyday cruelty and hatred of fake thuggery, gun violence and crime. This authority will protect the people's mind body and soul from all evil feelings, attitudes and actions as they move forward deeper and deeper into the century of the unknown. We will continue fighting against the evil and oppressive system of hopelessness, greed, disrespect, dishonour, and disunity on a daily basis without any end in sight for miles.

In the 21st century, We the People are now living and working in mentally and spiritually critical times that is very hard for some people to deal with in life so they remain non truth seekers aka evil doers working to make sure that evil is always over good in their lives. This BS type of mentality will lead to the impending mental and spiritual ruin that the angel named Lucifer aka Satan the Devil and his angels of destruction have been planning and working on for decades. In the 21st century, the people who are involved with the authority of respect, love and good intentions for one another will stop turning a blind eye to all the evidence on what fake thuggery, gun violence and crime continues to do to our communities and neighbourhoods which is the systematic killing and shooting of the unwanted people.

Truth and honour aka the Spirit of History is the only future that leads to Good over Evil happening in the future. We the People have to always try to strike for this consistency because there is a lack of communication and respect among the people, young and old who are not living with confidence in Good over Evil any more but they have a great comfort level when it comes to doing what's wrong and negative in life. It's time We the People stop underperforming mentally and spiritually on the battle field of Good over Evil and start supporting and promoting the Creator's original plan and Laws of Creation as an everyday activity like it's a 9-5 job.

The time has come for We the People to stop living and working in the oven and microwave of injustice and darkness aka planned doom that has cooked some people's mind, body and soul so they remain non truth seekers aka evil doers who will never submit to the authority of respect, love and good intentions for one another at no point in their life. SUBMISSION to this authority is a must; it's the only way to be mentally and spiritually successful in the battle of good intentions over evil spirits in the future.

BELIEVE IT OR NOT IT'S THE TRUTH!!

ALL RIGHTS RESERVED
01/16/2014

HEAVY ARTILLERY
By
Mr. Dave R. Queeley

In the 21st century, We the People have to be known as the NEW FREEDOM FIGHTERS who will only have the HEAVY ARTILLERY of respect, love and good intentions for one another on their minds in the battle of Good over Evil. This HEAVY ARTILLERY will be needed in the global mission of feeling the people, young and old mind, body and soul from the enemies iron grip. The enemies are hopelessness, greed, disrespect, dishonour and disunity. We the People have to remember this HEAVY ARTILLERY does not use any bullets like the ones that are always needed for the evil man made gadget of SELF destruction and death that fake thugs continue to use to commit all those senseless, random and unnecessary shootings and killings.

We are not what we once were people who had the HEAVY ARTILLERY of respect, love and good intentions for one another as an everyday activity. It was everyone's highest and top priority in life. We the People have not moved forward from seeing the number of people, young and old still without this HEAVY ARTILLERY of respect, love and good intentions for one another as part of their lives while on the evil battle field of injustice and darkness. Of course a lot of work still remains to be done so these people can finally wake up and respect the Creator's original plan and start following the Laws of Creation on a day to day basis without any timeouts or end in sight. These people have forgotten without the HEAVY ARTILLERY of respect, love and good intentions for one another on their minds and in their bodies and souls they will never be able to be the gatekeepers of Good over Evil.

In order to be a real true gatekeeper, an individual has to have discipline, faith and respect for the Creator's original plan. This will make sure the Laws of Creation will remain un-shattered by injustice and darkness aka planned doom. Being a real true gatekeeper will stop the dangerous and deadly divisions that the enemies who are hopelessness, greed, disrespect, dishonour and disunity continue to cause on a regular basis in our communities and neighbourhoods without any real true end and solution in sight. The people who are involved or have the HEAVY ARTILLERY of respect, love and good intentions for one another will distance themselves from anything that is evil and negative in life.

These people will never be involved in the glorification of Greed is good and hatred at no time in life. In the 21st century, the HEAVY ARTILLERY of respect, love and good intentions for one another will stop the people, young and old from shrinking back from Good over Evil like when a vampire sees or smells garlic. It will bring real true structure to the people, young and old who remain in mental and spiritual captivity lives once and for all. It will teach these people, it's time to have a collective resistance to all evil acts of injustice and darkness aka planned doom. It's time We the People stop working and living under the evil veil of secrecy, Greed is good and hatred where some people are not looking, wanting or working to leave these evil and negative feelings, attitudes and actions behind them on the battlefield of Good over Evil.

When this happens, life in our communities and neighbourhoods will once again be great without any mental and spiritual stress from the enemies who are hopelessness, greed, disrespect, dishonour and disunity. We have to always remember these enemies will never help preserve the mental and spiritual integrity of the people. Only try to destroy it on a daily basis. The HEAVY ARTILLERY of respect, love and good intentions for one another will get the people much more engaged in Good over Evil. It's time we change the way we do our mental and spiritual business. In the 21st century, We the People keep on forgetting injustice and darkness aka planned doom are capable of instigating wide spread hatred and keeps on turning our communities, neighbourhoods and societies upside down.

Greed is good has some people now absorbing the despicable behaviour and culture of injustice and darkness as an everyday activity in their lives because there is now a strong mental and spiritual critique that is All About the Benjamins aka the money, the root to all evil that happens in our communities and neighbourhoods and societies all around the world with no real true end in sight. We the People have to make sure the challenges and changes of life do not continue to affect the people's young and old minds, bodies and souls anymore in the 21st century. The HEAVY

ARTILLERY of respect, love and good intentions for one another are a huge adrenaline rush that will help prevent Greed is good, BLACK ON BLACK CRIME and hatred from being successful and prosperous in the future. It's a whole new level of conquering without a sword or one of those evil man made gadgets of destruction and death aka the GUN.

Greed is good and hatred is a refuge from the realities of life of Good over Evil , but there is also something else which is a wee bit more sinister and it's called BLACK ON BLACK CRIME, the first and last step to extinction happening. In the 21st century most people don't even smile at one another anymore; it's always the mean mugging," I don't give a damn" look that continues to keep them mentally and spiritually down in the pit of injustice and darkness aka planned doom. The HEAVY ARTILLERY of respect, love and good intentions for one another is always solid as a rock and nothing can stop it now from regaining control of the people's lives especially the ones who remain in mental and spiritual captivity. These people have to overstand that these positive feelings, attitudes and actions will always keep the Creator's original plan and following the Laws of Creation will always be on their mental and spiritual radar of life at all times.

They keep on forgetting without the HEAVY ARTILLERY of respect, love and good intentions for one another real true mental and spiritual captivity of injustice and darkness aka planned doom will continue to happen. In the 21st century there are lots of people that go through life from the cradle to the grave without ever expressing themselves and it's very sad to see this happening on a regular basis in our communities and neighbourhoods because some people are not fearful of being seen doing something evil, wrong and negative in life. The time has come to devote ourselves to fighting against and destroying the enemies of the HEAVY ARTILLERY of respect, love and good intentions for one another. These enemies are hopelessness, greed, disrespect, dishonour and disunity who are always on the battle field of Good over Evil causing mental and spiritual tension and havoc on a regular basis in our communities and neighbourhoods with no real true end in sight.

In the 21st century We the People have to always remember there is no end to learning about and practicing Good over Evil. Greed is good, BLACK ON BLACK CRIME and hatred have some people totally unprepared when it comes to being victorious in the battle of Good over Evil having the HEAVY ARTILLERY of respect, love and good intentions for one another in one's life is no good if you don't use it every day. Using it will help the people to stop being mentally and spiritually lost in the battle of Good over Evil at all times.

ALL RIGHTS RESERVED
01/18/2014

OUR STORY
By
Mr. Dave R. Queeley

Live from the streets of injustice and darkness also known as planned doom the Ourstory Recorder is reporting again. In the 21st century We the People must never forget on November 4, 2008, world history was made. A Mahogany man was voted in as the 44th President of the United States of America, from the slave ship to the White House. It's time Mahogany males see and know that with the Creator's love, words and help anything is possible and they can achieve anything they aspire to be in life, even being the President is possible.

1965 was the year that Mahogany people got the chance to cast a vote and it really meant something back then. Now 43 years later a Mahogany man is occupying the White House, a place where only Anglo-Saxon people of power lived and worked for hundreds of years. January 20, 2009, the day of the Inauguration, which is a day all Mahogany people must never forget to take honour in remembering all those people black and white who fought and died for the right to vote. That feeling of happiness and joy on November 4, 2008 will live on in OUR STORY forever, that anything is possible if you work hard for it without any shortcuts in life.

The 44th President still has to prove he is worthy of the White House and not just another Dixie pork barrel dealer politician of injustice and darkness also known as planned doom. A Mahogany man being elected was the vindication of the human spirit and the dignity of Good over Evil showing up at the ballot box. On November 4, 2008 it was one of those days that American was trying to live up to its creed that, "all men are created equally". It was a historical achievement in our history, but We the People are still perceived as the ones who will always pick the cotton, rather than the ones who owned the cotton plantation.

It's time We the People celebrate OUR STORY in any way we can, because OURSTORY is still being written every day that goes by. We have to keep on creating OURSTORY so that the new generation that has never watched ROOTS and AMISTAD before, never forget that before ROOTS, AMISTAD and a Mahogany man was elected to the White House, we were KINGS AND QUEENS. The time has come for Mahogany people to express their feelings about the fact that what many of them described and thought as impossible in their lifetime has finally come to pass; a Mahogany man will be living and working in the White House. In the 21st century We the People new motto should be, "don't buy where you cannot live or work and be treated as equals". We must always remember no one is advancing positive race relations talks between the people who are racist (the HAVES) and the people who are the sufferers of their evil feelings, attitudes and actions of hatred (the HAVE NOTS).

The people who are racist need to be informed that Greed is good and hatred is the mental and spiritual electric chair that symbolizes death all around the world. Not voting is always reliving the mental and spiritual humiliation of the past as slaves when we had no equality what so ever. Voting is sending a signal to the enemies of respect, love and good intentions for one another, "WE ARE NOT SLAVES ANYMORE." We the People are going to have to stand tall on the shoulders of all the giants and great Mahogany and Anglo-Saxon people who died and fought for this divine right to vote.

In OURSTORY, we must always remember the enemies of respect, love and good intentions for one another fear a world of Mahogany unity which will have world domination with the help to Good over Evil at all times. In the 21st century some people are saying, thinking and believing since a Mahogany man is in the White House, maybe he can finally fix OURSTORY and give the Mahogany people the forty acres and a mule they were promised centuries ago by the settlers of injustice and darkness by the people of power at that evil and negative time in OURSTORY.

We the People must never forget without respect, love and good intentions for one another, we will continue to be a people who are obsessed with petty needs, material greed and hatred. We the People have suffered brutalizing beatings for the right to vote, so why are we dying so fast trying to survive in the New World of injustice and darkness. We the People have to always remember one Mahogany man in the White House cannot fix centuries of oppression and discrimination, it will take the whole nation of Mahogany people seeking and serving ONE GOD, ONE AIM AND ONE DESTINY on a daily basis, only then Wilmot Blyden, Marcus Garvey, Malcolm X, Mahatma Ghandi and Martin Luther King Jr. would be happy men in their graves; who are now Resting In Peace because their sweat, blood and life has now finally paid off in full.

OURSTORY, IT'S TIME TO PROTECT IT!

ALL RIGHTS RESERVED
02/03/2014
Read on The Avalanche Radio Show on 02/05/2014

NATIVE BORN
By
Mr. Dave R. Queeley

It's time to bring the real true mental and spiritual heat. In the 21st century some NATIVE BORN people wish bad government and bad policies would leave us the hell alone because it's hurting and doing more harm than good to the future of NATIVE BORN people also known as Virgin Islanders. In the 21st century the hypocrisy of the people who are working for Joe Bogus aka the government and are in charge will always remain the problem to NATIVE BORN people being successful in their own home land. It's time for no more mental and spiritual drama because it's time to seek and serve respect, love and good intentions for one another on a regular basis without any more timeouts and blackouts happening.

We have to always remember glory be to the Creator for the Creator is love and never hate. The time has come for all NATIVE BBORN people to eliminate Greed is good, BLACK ON BLACK CRIME and hatred out of their lives once and for all. We have to remember all of the problems in our government system stem from several evil roots. Just to name a few, MONEY, SEX AND DRUGS; followed by Greed is good, hatred and SELFishness. Bad policies and bad government is all built on a bunch of lies. Until We the People acknowledge these lies we will continue to suffer being oppressed on a daily basis.

In the 21st century we are not paying attention to the heart beating everyday saying DO GOOD, DO GOOD, DO GOOD. NATIVE BORN people aka Virgin Islanders are now living and working in mediocrity. Sometimes they feel like their government system is now a brothel run by corruption, injustice and darkness aka planned doom. The evil people who are working for Joe Bogus aka the Government keep on forgetting that respect, love and good intentions for one another are the mental and spiritual capital of diversity and tolerance of one another on the battle field of Good over Evil at all times.

In the 21st century NATIVE BORN people now have a culture that has grown more and more accepting of Greed is good, BLACK ON BLAC CRIME and hatred. It's time to universally ban these evil and negative feelings, attitudes and actions of discrimination. We have to ground this BS mentality because we are still a people without full mental and spiritual equality in this New World of injustice and darkness. In the 21st century having respect, love and good intentions for one another will make sure We the People have the mental and spiritual resistance to stop being relegated to society's back rooms and shadows of injustice and darkness as we move forward into the century of the unknown.

Those people who do not remember the mistakes of the past are all destined to repeat them in the future. NATIVE BORN people are the ones who are under employed not outsiders they can come from wherever they use to live with their bogus qualifications and get a good paying job in

Joe Bogus aka the government at $100,000 and over while NATIVE BORN people continue to suffer everyday under economic pressure and oppression from the people who are now in charge as our policy makers. NATIVE BORN people need to perform one of the largest anti-government system protest that the world and our history has ever seen before it's too damn late for any protest to work.

We the People cannot give up on whether the mental and spiritual momentum that is needed for this anti-government system to work could be kept up or if it has the staying power to force real true change and reform in our communities and neighbourhoods. The spark for this protest will be all the allegations of wide spread corruption, fraud bribe taking and refusing to let the people know who the criminals are that took part in the 6.9 million dollar heist without a gun that took place in 2011 which is now the greatest embarrassment to America's so called Paradise image. In the 21st century, NATIVE BORN people are facing outrageous rents and mortgage payments, electrical oppression, expensive food and gas prices on a daily basis because they do not have the money to keep on greasing the wheels of injustice and darkness.

When the Our Story Recorder turns on the radio or T.V. and read the newspaper he feels ashamed of how low and far off his homeland and town has fallen off the map of Good over Evil. This has now created a society with a culture of low expectations from life. The Our Story Recorder wants to take our broken homes, churches and schools and turn them back into a mental and spiritual paradise of respect, love and good intentions for one another. In the 21st century, liberty, equality and freedom are not a part of NATIVE BORN peoples world like being stupid, evil and greedy people. We the People must understand there is always a number of circumstances and conditions that can lead to this mentality happening in someone's life. Sometimes it's mental and spiritual poverty and joblessness that are a major cause to this social ill, conflict and problem. Waiting to fix this evil mentality will turn into a really bad disaster that will need F.E.M.A.'s help in the future to bring back law and order.

This type of B.S. mentality is never a positive step forward in the battle of Good over Evil. The truth is, it continues to tarnish our communities and neighbourhoods as a safe place to live and work and visit, night or day. The suffering and pain going on in the trenches of injustice and darkness have gone unnoticed by Joe Bogus aka the government for too many decades without any help in sight. There is no explanation for why the constant lack of respect, love and good intentions for one another continue to exist in our communities and neighbourhoods .

This BS mentality continues to lead to the wild goose chase of SELF destruction and death happening on a regular basis; rather than bringing back respect, love and good intentions for one another for all NATIVE BORN people once and for all which will be a historical moment in OUR STORY!

ALL RIGHTS RESERVED
01/21/2014

G-ANGELS
By
Mr. Dave R. Queeley

TURNING IT ON FOR REAL, SO HATERS BEWARE.

Here we go again the Our Story Recorder is turning on the faucet of truth and honour with help from his G-ANGELS who will be hoping it floods out the evil house of injustice and darkness aka planned doom. A darkness that some people have been working and living in for years. The Our Story recorder knows what he signed up for when he became a truth seeker on the battle field of Good over Evil. He became a soul writer who remains old fashioned with this thought provoking social oratories. The Our Story Recorder has surrounded himself with trust worthy and hard working individuals who are G-ANGELS; people who understand that we are going to get a million doors slammed closed in our faces, but if we have the right mental and spiritual product and grind we will make it to the top.. No matter who is in our way to the top of truth and honour, here we come.

These trust worthy and hard working individuals who are my G-ANGELS know what time it is. It's time to be victorious in the battle of Good over Evil and for all those who possess a passion for mental, spiritual and social justice aka justice for every day that goes by. The Our Story Recorder is an avid supporter and promoter of the preventions of fake thuggery, gun violence and crime from its continued growth in our communities and neighbourhoods. Some people will oppose changing and reforming these evil feelings, attitudes and action that keeps our communities and neighbourhoods mentally and spiritually divided. We the People have to fix all the Crime-ridden areas and parts of our communities and neighbourhoods, if we want to be mentally and spiritually victorious in the battle of Good over Evil.

Back in the good old days of peace, freedom and unity our communities and neighbourhoods use to be the village that raised, nurtured and protected the children and young people from the enemies who are hopelessness, greed, disrespect, dishonour, and disunity. But now, in the 21st century there are places where they lose their lives on a regular basis for no good and godly reason under the sun, moon and stars. The Our Story Recorder and his G-ANGELS knows instead of throwing the book at the mentally and spiritually troubled young people and children when they get in trouble with the law and the injustice system (courts). We the People have to do our part everyday that goes by to give young people and children a real true second chance at life to get back on the right and positive track of Good over Evil. But first we need more examples of acts of respect, love and good intentions for one another happening every day so these mentally and spiritually troubled people can see there is a better way out to eternal hell fire that sometimes leads to the pit of doom (jail or prison).

SELF destruction and death happening some times because there is no campaign to bring back respect, love and good intentions for one another as an everyday activity back into our communities and neighbourhoods. Every day We the People pay the price for not supporting and promoting the Creator's original plan and for not following the Laws of Creation. This price that we pay is all the senseless, random and unnecessary killings and shootings that continue to happen on a daily basis without any real true end in sight for miles. The sunshine of Good over Evil doesn't shine brightly anymore in some people's mind, body and soul at no point in life.

It's time to declare a war on fake thuggery, gun violence and crime and propose a real true return to the Creator's original plan which is Good will conquer Evil and Love will triumph over Hate, and to make sure following the Laws of Creation is everyone's top and highest priority in life. These positive feelings, attitudes and actions will help the people young and old remain among the upper echelon of the mental and spiritual society of Good over Evil and they will have no DNA of injustice and darkness aka planned doom in their mind, body and soul. In the 21st century many non truth seekers aka evil doers continue to fear the final battle of Good over Evil for world supremacy that will finally signal the end of their evil civilization of injustice and darkness as they now know it.

It will be destroyed. Only they respect, love and good intentions for one another will stop declining in our communities and neighbourhoods and life will improve at all levels once and for all. The people, who are not involved with respect, love and good intentions for one another keep on forgetting these positive feelings, attitudes and actions never age, they get better with time and they will never keep anyone off balance or off beat in life while on the battle field of Good over Evil. In the 21st century the Our Story Recorder and his G-ANGELS knows what has to unite We the People is the hard work for the deep and abiding belief in the dignity and loyalty of Good over Evil. We have to always remember everyone has the right to dream and then have the opportunity for those dreams to be realized. We have to finally realized that respect, love and good intentions for one another are a fraternity that anyone can join and you don't need any money to pay dues; all you need to join is to be a real true supporter and promoter of the Creator's original plan and following the Laws of Creation have to be any everyday activity.

The time has come for We the People to start implementing these positive feelings, attitudes and actions day to day as a choice and not just lip service that only has the evil echo of injustice and darkness attached to it. Injustice and darkness will never be involved with alleviating mental and spiritual poverty out of our communities and neighbourhoods at no time. The soft mental and spiritual society of welfarism does not restore the inner Messiah and true meaning about what life is all about, which is to always be on the front lines of the battle of Good over Evil at all times. The Our Story Recorder and his G-ANGELS knew their calling in life was much higher than just being an evil doer aka bad man or non truthseeker.

They knew once they became truth seekers they could inspire the people young and old to return to having respect, love and good intentions for one another on a regular basis as we move forward, deeper and deeper into the century of the unknown. We the People have to always remember the enemies of respect, love and good intentions for one another will never allow the people to exercise their divine right to be treated as a real true role model, leader and super hero to the young people and children who remain mentally and spiritually troubled while on the battlefield of Good over Evil at all times. Respect, love and good intentions for one another will make sure these mentally and spiritually troubled people will not have any more sympathy for Greed is good, BLACK ON BLACK CRIME and hatred at no point in life.

They always have to remember G-ANGELS are not gangsters; they are real true doers of the word; who knows there is no substitute to the fulfilment of Good over Evil. The Our Story Recorder and his G-ANGELS knows it's better to shoot from the lips and pen and not the GUN.

The GUN takes lives and the PEN and LIPS do not.
WISE UP AND BECOME A G-ANGEL.

ALL RIGHTS RESERVED
01/23/2014

THREATENING OUR PATHWAY
By
Mr. Dave R. Queeley

There are no right or left turns from the PATHWAY that was already laid out by our ancestors, that's why we have to keep the momentum of Good over Evil and look to accelerate it every single day that goes by. There is no more waiting to accelerate it or we've got to take a mental and spiritual pause from promoting and supporting Good over Evil. In the 21st century some people hope and pray we accelerate this progress ASAP. We are no longer just looking for viability, but we are looking for respect, growth and leadership in the operation of Good over Evil all around the world of injustice and darkness aka planned doom.

The message of Good over Evil has to be clear and consistent worldwide, only then respect, love and good intentions for one another will become a global luxury for all. It's time to focus on innovative ideas and solutions that will add real true value to these feelings, attitudes, and actions that are very important steps for anyone who wants to be mentally and spiritually victorious in the battle of life, which is Good over Evil. In the 21st century it's now impossible to gauge the people, young and old mindset to how far they will go to keep injustice and darkness alive in their lives. They keep on forgetting anyone who feeds off negativity will never be mentally and spiritually successful in the future. They will remain searching for ways out of the bottomless pit of mental and spiritual emptiness everyday that goes by in the 21st century.

Greed is good, BLACK ON BLACK CRIME and hatred continues THREATENING OUR PATHWAY to world peace, freedom and unity in our communities and neighbourhoods without a real true mental and spiritual fight from the people who say they are involved with Good over Evil at all times. These people keep on forgetting being involved with Good over Evil or having the heavy artillery of respect, love and good intentions for one another in their lives as an everyday activity is never a crime. Wherever this heavy artillery is not allowed or practiced Greed is good, BLACK ON BLACK CRIME and hatred continues to flourish with no end in sight. Our communities and neighbourhoods are on the brink of mental and spiritual catastrophe. If these Evil feelings, attitudes and actions continue, it will lead to SELF destruction, death and maybe extinction happening in the future.

It's time to pick up the heavy artillery of respect, love and good intentions for one another and start defending the family , the Creator's original plan and following the Laws of Creation on a day to day basis until victory is won on the battlefield of Good over Evil. Nothing else in life is that serious for mankind to take a life. Without this heavy artillery there will never be any permanent mental and spiritual repair going on n our communities and neighbourhoods. It's only temporary repair going on because there is no SELF sacrifice from the people, young and old. This heavy artillery which needs to be used to crack criminals aka fake thugs skulls, will persist and maybe it will likely wake them up to stop them from ending up severely injured and maybe dead due to they are involved with Greed is good, BLACK ON BLACK CRIME and hatred aka unjust treatment.

These evil feelings, attitudes and actions continue THREATENING OUR PATHWAY to Good over Evil in the future, because life is not a game or comic book. Some people continue to take a mellower approach and stay away from vigilantism against these evil feelings, attitudes and actions that keeps fake thuggery, gun violence and crime alive in our communities and neighbourhoods. We the People must always remember these evil feelings, attitudes and actions keeps the murder and incarceration rate very high as the days go by. They are never a powerful presence of Good over Evil at no point in time. In the 21st century some people are not willing to accept and increase pressure on our communities and neighbourhoods to make the mental and spiritual changes and reform that is needed to be successful in the future and to stop letting injustice an darkness continue THREATIENING OUR PATHWAY of Good over Evil.

Until We the People get together and cleanup our acts and become real true leaders of our families, fake thuggery, gun violence and crime will continue to happen in our communities and neighbourhoods on a daily basis. We keep on forgetting that life should not consist of more pain, more sorrow and more condolence to families who have lost a loved one. But it should be about spreading more love, more respect and more good intentions for one another every single day that go by. There are a lot of mental and spiritual differences in our communities, neighbourhoods and world and not a lot of ways to be effective and victorious in the battle of Good over Evil. But to be mentally and spiritually successful, you have to figure out what's best for you and work to achieve it to the best of your mental and spiritual ability.

That's what being involved with Good over Evil is all about. It will stop the enemies of respect, love and good intentions for one another from THREATENING OUR PATHWAY for the top of TRUTH AND HONOR aka the Spirit of Ourstory. Truth and Honour have one lifestyle and it's called Keeping It Real in deed and not just lip service. But the one thing that draws and keeps the enemies of respect, love and good intentions for one another together is the mythology of Greed is good and hatred is alright as long as it's BLACK ON BLACK CRIME. Some people will be reluctant to let go of the evil feelings, attitudes and actions. They keep on saying to themselves," I cannot leave it behind ", because it's very good to them and there is no shortage of evil things to do trying to get rich or die trying.

These people keep on forgetting that respect, love and good intentions for one another will expand their enlightenment knowledge and understanding. It's time to seek and serve Good over Evil as an everyday activity moving forward deeper and deeper into the century of the unknown. This enlightenment knowledge and understanding will stop them from tuning into war and hate mongers who have sold their mind, body and soul to injustice and darkness for nothing. Having respect, love and good intentions for one another is simply not on their radar screen of Good over Evil.

In the 21st century some people are saying and thinking, how long are We the People going to continue to disrespect and hate the PATHWAY that was already paved with mental and spiritual gold by our ancestors, centuries ago. This PATHWAY OF GOLD is called Good over Evil at all times.

ALL RIGHTS RESERVED
01/28/2014

POWER IN MOTIVATING PEOPLE (P.I.M.P.)

By
Mr. Dave R. Queeley

There is a big misconception that We the People are not trying very hard to break down the evil walls of fake thuggery, gun violence and crime in the 21st century. But that's a big lie because there are some people who are always on the mental and spiritual battlefield trying to have the POWER IN MOTIVATING PEOPLE to think and do better in life while on the battlefield of Good over evil. When We the People start thinking and doing better in life, this will usher in the real true end of fake thuggery, gun violence and crime.

The time has come to hit these evil feelings, attitudes and actions over the head with the sledgehammer of respect, love and good intention for one another once and for all. The people who continue to have these evil feelings, attitudes and action in their lives are just mental and spiritual appetizers for injustice and darkness aka planned doom. These people will always have no state of consciousness when it comes to good over Evil. They keep on forgetting that Truth and Honour aka the Spirit of History is the diary of life and the journey of Good over Evil is very rewarding, mentally and spiritually. It will help the people find their way out of the mental and spiritual fog that is so thick they can't breathe and find their way back on the right pathway that leads to the promoting and supporting of the Creator's original plan and following the Laws of Creation as an everyday activity.

These positive feelings, attitudes and actions will make sure the people start seeing their communities, neighbourhoods and world with brand new eyes, everything will be so clear, they will not continue to keep one foot in the grave by being involved with Greed is good, BLACK ON BLACK CRIME and hatred. Some people keep on saying, thinking and believing life is too short, so why care or give a damn about anything like that in life. These people keep on forgetting that the POWER IN MOTIVATING PEOLE does not come from being involved with Greed is good, BLACK ON BLACK CRIME and hatred, which only leads to SELF destruction and death.

This type of mentality continues to exist and happen because of the people's sluggish mental and spiritual growth in returning to having respect, love, justice and good intentions for one another as their highest and top priority in life. The decline of these feelings, attitudes and actions continues to hurt our communities, neighbourhoods and world on a daily basis with no end in sight for miles. The POWER TO MOTIVATE PEOPLE is to make sure they do not remain powerless at eliminating fake thuggery, gun violence and crime out of their lives. This power will help liberate the people from the cages of injustice and darkness. That they have been working and living in for decades.

It's time to curb the outward manifestations of these evil feelings, attitudes and actions in our communities, neighbourhoods and world. In the 21st century the people, young and old judge each other by what they wear and what they look like. This type of mentality is not a good example of Good over Evil. This evil mentality keeps the people not thinking about that, there are not equal rights under the laws of injustice and darkness for the people, especially if they are Mahogany. The people in our communities, neighbourhoods and world whose good deeds and intentions will inspire the people who remain in mental and spiritual captivity to free their mind, body and soul from injustice and darkness; because bad deeds and intentions get all the media coverage in the 21st century.

Respect, love and good intentions for one another will make sure these people are doing better and stronger mentally and spiritually every day that goes by. They will love being in a positive atmosphere working and living for Good over Evil, knowing that nothing good in life comes easy at no point in life. Respect, love and good intentions for one another will give them the DIVINE VISION to finally destroy fake thuggery, gun violence and crime, so that their existence does not continue to be in injustice and darkness. But it will be in the mental and spiritual heaven of Good over Evil which has the POWER TO MOTIVATE PEOPLE to live right and be positive on the battlefield of injustice and darkness as the days go by.

We the People must always understand that POWER IN MOTIVATING PEOPLE is all about the declaration on the mental and spiritual elimination of fake thuggery, gun violence and crime from our adopted new world of injustice and darkness. Respect, love and good intentions for one another are the most valuable tool that is needed to eliminate these evil feelings, attitudes and actions out of our communities, neighbourhoods and world that has caused mental and spiritual suffering and poverty to happen on a regular basis. POWER IN MOTIVATING PEOPLE is all about the positive impact on our communities, neighbourhoods and world. It's never involved in negativity the people who have the POWER to MOTIVATE the PEOPLE are very allergic to Greed is good, BLACK ON BLACK CRIME and hatred. They know these evil feelings, attitudes and actions will never help them to be mentally and spiritually victorious in the battle of the Good over Evil.

These feelings, attitudes and actions have turned some people into C.E.O.'s of 666, injustice and darkness while on the battle field of Good over Evil. We the People have to be more mentally and spiritually aggressive in promoting and supporting the return to having respect, love and good intentions for one another back into our communities, neighbourhoods and world. In the 21st century we have to take the warning from the Creator more seriously than ever before in life. Greed is good, BLACK ON BLACK CRIME and hatred are the most bold-faced excuses that some people use to not do what's right and positive in life.

We the People have to seek the death penalty against fake thuggery, gun violence and crime on a daily basis. We can now accuse some people of betraying the Creator's original plan and Laws of Creation by being involved with these evil feeling, attitudes and actions. These people have forgotten that the lack of remorse equals premeditation. This premeditation only keeps injustice and darkness alive in our communities, neighbourhoods and world. It's time to eliminate the evil stench of Greed is good, BLACK ON BLACK CRIME and hatred from killing and hurting our innocent civilians getting to the top of Truth and Honour aka the Spirit of History is not an easy thing for some people to do in life because they have sold their mind, body and soul to the enemies which are hopelessness, disrespect, dishonour, and disunity.

They will never find the POWER to MOTIVATE the PEOPLE to be mentally and spiritually victorious in the battle of Good over Evil. We the People need to stay ready with the POWER to MOTIVATING one another to be victorious in the battle of Good over Evil. There isn't any time for getting ready. NOW IS THE TIME!

EARN YOUR P.I.M.P.!

ALL RIGHTS RESERVED
02/03/2014
Read on The Avalanche Radio Show on 02/05/2014

187 IN THE VI
AKA STOP THE INSANITY
By
Mr. Dave R. Queeley

RIP Kervin Williams, another victim of a senseless 187.
GONE BUT NOT FORGOTTEN. 187 IS THE POLICE RADIO CODE FOR MURDER.

187 is casting a bad shadow over the VI. ALL Virgin Islanders need to get back to their cultural roots of keeping it real and they've got to make the hard decision of returning to having manners, respect, love, and good intentions for one another and remember it's part of a crucial strategy aimed at reducing 187, gun violence and disrespect in their communities and neighbourhoods. It's unquestionably a big step in the right direction of PROMOTING or SPONSORING the Creator's original plan of Good will conquer evil and Love will triumph over hate.

187 in the VI is now the number one reason why young people or their family members are losing their lives and not of old age, which is called NATURAL CAUSES. Manners, love, and good intentions for one another use to be in all Virgin Islanders DNA. In the 21st century their DNA is now made up of disrespect, violent behaviour and

dishonour. Virgin Islanders cannot simply magically think things are going to get better or 187 is going to stop or just disappear. It's time ALL Virgin Islanders stand shoulder to shoulder on the frontlines and find a way to take evil spirits out of their lives and stopping young people from relocating to the cemetery or life in prison. YOUNG PEOPLE must realize "A PEOPLE UNITED BY MANNERS, LOVE, AND GOOD INTENTIONS FOR ONE ANOTHER WILL NEVER BE DEFEATED by 187 in the battle of Good and Evil.

187 has now achieved legendary proportions and it's now incarcerating young people at an astronomical rate into the pit of doom. The VI now has one of the highest per capita 187 rates of any jurisdictions under the US flag and that's very bad for such a small territory to have such a high 187 rate. Something is seriously wrong with the people living here who are committing all these senseless, random and unnecessary acts of 187. All Virgin Islanders have the moral authority to complain about how far 187, gun violence and crime will go, IT'S TIME TO STOP THE INSANITY! Virgin Islanders are now living in perpetual fear of being victimized by or witness to a violent crime of injustice. 187, gun violence and crime continues to be the number one source of ruining for life in the VI. All Virgin Islanders should be sued or charged

with malpractice of the Creator's original plan and laws of Creation, the true- lifeline to eternal life.

Virgin Islanders now have to face their mental and spiritual demons and remember it takes lots of courage to walk away and it's very easy to pull the trigger and commit 187. There are some Virgin Islanders who are now confident that they are headed in the right direction if they return to having manners, respect, love, and good intentions for one another. They must always remember it's their job to keep the recovery moving and to get it stronger and to accelerate the Creator's original plan that is needed so desperately in the 21st century. 187, gun violence and crime is a major change from a generation ago where Virgin Islanders had love and respect for one another. Disrespect ,violent behaviour and dishonour is now the driving force behind the surge of 187 now taking place in the VI in the 21st century. Violent behaviour, disrespect and dishonour continue to embarrass the VI in the public eyes by continuing to make the front page of the newspaper, radio, or television for the senseless, random and unnecessary acts of mayhem and 187. The police keep on promising to unveil an agenda to fighting violent crime and so far the VI still has nothing.

Their crime fighting prescription is simple, WAIT UNTIL THE SHOTS STOP FIRING THEN GO TO THE CRIME SCENE…(to see who got 187 or what has happened.) The police are here to protect and serve the citizens of the VI, not to help execute them. The current crime fighting strategy isn't working and it's costing human blood or body organs to be spilled or flow in the streets.

187, gun violence ,disrespect and dishonour continue to beat Virgin Islanders into submission to accepting Satan's angels of destruction as God. Virgin Islanders now need to be hooked up to the IV of having manners, love, respect and good intentions for one another and they must realize returning to these positive feelings, attitudes and actions is not something that stays stagnant, it keeps moving like a river or a mighty stream. All Virgin Islanders need to latch on to the tantalizing reality that if 187, gun violence ,disrespect and dishonour continue to grow huge and out of control, the whole Virgin Island Territory will become an endangered species that needs Federal Protection.

The American Paradise has quickly become the American 187 slums.

187 IN THE VI = STOP THE INSANITY

ALL RIGHTS RESERVED
September 23, 2010

187 IN THE VI II
AKA
THE BARREL OF THE GUN
By
Mr. Dave R. Queeley

Once again 187 is the police radio code for murder.

The first ten years of the 21st century has been the most murderous decade in the VI's recorded history all because of the barrel of the gun. Dying of natural causes at an old age is nowhere to be found today, 187 is number one. In the 30's, 40's, 50's and the 60's the barrel of the gun was not killing Virgin Islanders as fast as it's now happening in the 21st century. It's a sad reality that the barrel of the gun is the number one cause of death of Virgin Islanders young and old. Some Virgin Islanders are hoping and praying that they don't 3peat while watching their communities and neighbourhoods disintegrate into havens for crime and violence ruled by the barrel of the gun. The people who break the law has become more and more brazen doing whatever violent crime they are going to commit in broad day light. They must remember GANGS DON'T REPRESENT PEACE OR LOVE. They represent war, life in prison or death. Being murder(187) is a scenario all Virgin Islanders are faced with everyday as the sale of illegal weapons sky rocket through the ceiling and this is one fact that must be addressed quickly, before it's an all out civil war. Time for kill or be killed.

The police and politicians are not doing much in the way of stopping the sale of illegal weapons and bullets of evil on the streets of their communities and neighbourhoods. Virgin Islanders now have to fight or face the mindset that is prevalent wherever you may go, St. Croix, St. Thomas, or St. John that politicians or the police department and it's officers cannot be trusted at no time at all because they are all bloodsucking double agents and war criminals who are sworn to protect and serve; that is still left to be seen in the 21st century. Real political solutions or policing is critical to repairing the damage that the illegal barrel of the gun continues to leave behind in the Virgin Islands. Some people now want to know; Why a Virgin Islander needs an A-47 or an R-15? The VI does not have any forests or jungles for hunting. A Virgin Islander who owns an automatic weapon only has it for one use and that's usually always 187 and nothing else. Virgin Islanders are now consuming more bullets of evil from the barrel of the gun than ever before and they are losing their lives at an alarming rate.
Considering how many people have lost their lives since the beginning of the 21st century to the barrel of the gun, if they just look and listen to the traditional sources of information (newspaper,

radio, television) and Virgin Islanders will see and hear the evidence against illegal weapons in the VI.

It's time to sever the connection between 187 and the barrel of the gun because if the 187 rates continue to rise year after year, the VI will whittle away until there is nothing left but dead bodies. It's a grim reminder to Virgin Islanders that life here in the islands has changed from bad to worst. The barrel of the gun is now described as the all-powerful monster of death in the Virgin Islands.

Virgin Islanders now need to build a real true conglomerate of having manners, love, respect and good intentions for one another to fight in the battle of GOOD OVER EVIL if they want to see a decline in the use of the barrel of the gun to commit 187. Some Virgin Islanders are hoping and praying that young people will grow tired of the echo chamber of the barrel of the gun and return to having manners, respect, love, and good intentions for one another. Returning to these positive feelings, attitudes and actions will make young people feel weak and unmanly or unwomanly but it's a start to solving their mental and spiritual problem that continue to cause them to commit 187 with the barrel of the gun. All Virgin Islanders have to remember returning to manners, respect, love, and good intentions for one another will create a window of opportunity to find true solutions or to talk about what can be done to stopping all the random, senseless and unnecessary 187 and assaults with or without a deadly weapon.

Virgin Islanders must realize that reducing the ballooning 187 rates is necessary to surviving another five centuries. Greed, selfishness, and disrespect continue to mastermind all the random senseless and unnecessary 187 and assaults with or without a deadly weapon. All Virgin Islanders young and old must remember that taking one human life is like taking all life because there is no self-defense law in the court of the Creator's eyes because the number six commandments is THOU SHALL NOT KILL.

BUYING OR OWNING AN AUTOMATIC WEAPON = 187 IN THE VI

ALL RIGHTS RESERVED
9-27-2010

CHEATING
by
Mr. Dave R. Queeley

This is dedicated to all the people, who has been cheated on.
I AM A VICTIM.

SO, WHO FEELS IT KNOWS IT, STOP CHEATING.

CHEATING is the cardinal sin, and it's a mindblower for some people in a relationship. It's a feeling that can never be repaired. They keep on forgetting the key element of true love is to feel safe with the other person and to be able to trust them no matter what.

CHEATING is a total disrespect of the other person's feelings, love and good intentions.

CHEATING is a slap in the face to self-love and self-respect.

CHEATING will take no prisoners, because it's the number one source of dishonour, disrespect and destruction in a relationship.

CHEATING creates anger issues that sometimes leads to all kinds of abuse. Men must always remember, you can't beat a woman at the cheating game. They are the boss of all bosses in the world in that department women must remember when a man is cheating, he makes excuses for his behaviour and actions.

CHEATING is always the main disappointment in a relationship. Sometimes the death sentence to a lot of good relationships.

CHEATING is something most men and women can't handle, and they sometimes lose their minds and check out on life.

CHEATING is unacceptable behaviour in a relationship, nothing good comes from cheating only disrespect, dishonour and disunity comes from cheating.

CHEATING is like badminton, it's back and forth.

CHEATING is a temporary solution to whatever problems men and women may face in any relationship. Women sometimes say they cheat because they're men wouldn't listen or care enough. Men sometimes cheat because it's a deep ingrained part of their life. Men and women who cheat must always remember, KARMA is a serious thing.

CHEATING is playing the game of life unfair.
CHEATING will never be right.
CHEATERS NEVER PROSPER!

ALL RIGHTS RESERVED
September 24, 2011.

Read on The Avalanche Radio Show on 01/16/2010 at 5 PM 105 JAMZ.
The first one of ALL TURN UP!!

STILL CHEATING
Still a Victim
By
Mr. Dave R. Queeley

The truth shall set you free at all times in life. Real love, respect and good intentions is not a game, it's very hard to find it in the 21st century.

CHEATING has destroyed so many people's confidence in the opposite sex. These attitudes, feelings and actions keep hopelessness, disrespect, dishonour and disunity alive in their lives with no true end in sight for miles.

CHEATING has these same people continuing to attend the church of the poisoned mind, body and soul like it's something good to be doing in life.

CHEATING is all about making plans to do someone you say you love and respect wrong. That's not right at all.

CHEATING is all about one person not thinking about the other person's needs, feelings and the comfort of their relationship reaching for the skies which has no limits to it.

CHEATING always has the people who are involved with it suffering mentally, emotionally and spiritually in silence, because it will never help good win the battle over evil.

CHEATING is the attitudes, feelings and actions of the people who are always starving for emotional and physical affection from someone other than their partner.

CHEATERS do not play by the rules of love, respect and good intentions, but instead they play by the rules of illusion which requires all the mental and spiritual ruthlessness, they can muster in life.

CHEATING is never a feeling of incredible love between partners, but a feeling of incredible miscommunication between partners.

CHEATING keeps the people who are involved with it off-balance mentally and spiritually and it shows that the person who is doing it does not know how to be a good partner in life.

CHEATERS are never good partners, because a good partner in life never cheats. They tell the truth no matter if it hurts your feelings because without love, respect and good intentions. They easily succumb to the destructive and evil forces of injustice and darkness that continues to whirl around them every day.

CHEATING is never a feeling of emotional satisfaction, because some of the people who are involved with it sometimes regret their actions. It often times makes the situation worse.

CHEATING leaves deep emotional scars that can have lifelong implications on some people's mind, body and soul.

CHEATING is an unspeakable mental and spiritual crime against your partner.

CHEATING is the true image of self destruction and death of a relationship.

CHEATING is a hurting feeling inside that some people can never get rid of or overcome in life. It haunts them for the rest of their lives mentally and spiritually.

CHEATING will never lead to mental and spiritual perfection becoming a part of the people who are involved with it because it has a monopoly on hopelessness, disrespect, dishonour and disunity. It's never a hallelujah moment in life.

I am still a victim and cheaters still will never prosper in life. Truth always have a way of winning in the end.

ALL RIGHTS RESERVED
May 20, 2013

Read on The Avalanche Radio Show on 05/20/2013.

MORE CHEATING

The knowledge continues to why I am still a victim.
By
Mr. Dave R. Queeley

CHEATING is back by popular demand. I had to deliver another jewel. This one is dedicated to all the people who cherished the first two.

Especially the female who stuck them on her bedroom door, so her boyfriend can read and see them every day, this one's for you. Sorry brother, I am just keeping it real 100%. The truth shall set you free.

The people who **CHEAT** does not always have their partner on their mind at all times. If they did, they would not be playing this deceiving game that keeps them mentally and spiritually empty, without true love, respect and good intentions in their lives.

CHEATERS are always people whose self esteem, self pride, self-love and self-respect are at a very low level in their lives.

CHEATERS are never soldiers of good intentions over evil spirits, but they are always soldiers of hopelessness, disrespect, dishonour and disunity which never brings to life, "until death do us part" kind of love to their relationships for real.

CHEATERS keep on forgetting their attitudes, feelings

and actions continue to lead to jealousy, hatred and sometimes death happening.

CHEATERS continue to make sure love, respect and good intentions are out of their picture of life, which is a very bad sign for any future relationship.

CHEATERS will never have any mental and spiritual etiquette involved in their lives at no 1 point in time.

CHEATERS have forgotten that their forefathers were never involved in this type of disrespectful and negative behaviour at any time in history.

CHEATERS are always the number one supporters and promoters of self-hate and adultery.

CHEATERS are always ostracized in our communities and neighbourhoods for their actions that are always unfair to their partners in life.

CHEATERS will never be welcomed into the paradise of truth and honour with open arms or with a big smile in the future.

CHEATERS will never embrace the big picture of life, which is good intentions must conquer and triumph over all evil spirits no matter what happens in these perilous times.

CHEATERS have more problems and hang-ups than a telemarketer on the job from 9 to 5.

CHEATERS continue to misinterpret the Creators original

plan and laws of creation as something negative to be involved with in this lifetime. They keep on forgetting these attitudes, feelings and actions are the psychological anchor of good intentions over evil spirits at all times.

CHEATERS will never prosper because there is no real antidote for cheating that exists in the world.

STOP IT NOW, IT'S NO GOOD!

ALL RIGHTS RESERVED
06/02/2013.

INSIGHT
By
Mr. Dave R. Queeley

SAM I AM, I HOPE YOU LOVE THIS REAL TALK

In the 21st century We the People are not serious about our mental and spiritual sobriety, so they keep on getting drunk on the liquor or wine of injustice and darkness aka planned doom with no end in sight. According to the dictionary, INSIGHT means the capacity to discern the real true nature of things. The people who are involved with insight will embrace and assist in the spreading of the teaching of the Creator's original plan and following the Laws of Creation ensuring it is always on their minds and in their bodies and souls as an everyday activity.

INSIGHT keeps the people mentally and spiritually calm to carry on the battle of Good over Evil at all times no matter where they are in the world. INSIGHT is like the Serenity Prayer aka Alcoholics Anonymous Prayer," God grant me the Serenity to accept the things I cannot change and the Courage to change the things I can change and the Wisdom to know the difference." INSIGHT is having a firm grip on the truth and honour aka the spirit of history and it's never involved in self hate.

It's always involved in promoting and supporting having manners, respect, love and good intentions for one another as an everyday activity. The people who have INSIGHT knows the same mental and spiritual struggle they now have in this life is the same struggle as when our ancestors were alive. Nothing has changed, it's just a new look to deceive the people that Greed is Good and Hatred is alright as long as it's Black on Black Crime. Greed is Good has to be going out of style like the 8 track tape player because it's a phoney mentality that leads to mental and spiritual sickness, destruction and sometimes death happening.

In the 21st century hatred will not plague We the People no more in life if we have INSIGHT to make sure Good over Evil happens and the people will never find themselves between a rock and a hard place. INSIGHT will turn these people into bonafide supporters and promoters of the Creator's original plan and Laws of Creation as an everyday activity moving deeper and deeper into the 21st century of the unknown.

INSIGHT will make sure We the People never give up on Good over Evil at any time and unlock the secret weapon that lays deep inside every human being waiting to burst out. These secret weapons are having manners, respect, love and good intentions for one another and they will never lead to mental and spiritual extinction at no point in life.

INSIGHT has no limitations and it helps everyone who is involved with it tap into their internal energies of Good over Evil at all times. It's the first step to stop being an embarrassment to the game of life.

INSIGHT

ALL RIGHTS RESERVED
12-29-2013
Read on The Avalanche Radio Show on 01/27/2014

LIFE
By
Mr. Dave R. Queeley

LIFE in our sick society is getting worse as the days go by. We the People continue to see and watch our offspring die from an overdose of mental and spiritual poverty and hatred.

LIFE is now a reflection of this continued mental and spiritual abuse, pain and suffering on a daily basis.

LIFE as a negative and evil person is never easy because it's full of extreme lows and sometimes highs.

LIFE in our communities continue to be threatened and endangered by hopelessness, greed, disrespect, dishonour, and disunity on a daily basis.

LIFE is mentally and spiritually difficult for the people who are homeless and know nothing about having manners, love, respect and good intentions for one another.

LIFE is the regard for one's own happiness and success.

It's all about staying in one's mental and spiritual lane trying to see the paradise of truth and honour that have streets of gold.

LIFE has no dress rehearsal because the camera keeps on rolling until you see the credits at the end, which means death.

It's a gift from the Creator and it needs to be cherished like money.

LIFE is never about being delusional; it's always full of truth, honour and loyalty all day, every day.

It's never about being powerless against evil and negative feelings, attitudes and actions.

LIFE is all about accurately representing the Creators original plan and following the laws of creation until prophecy is fulfilled in the future.

It's never suppose to reflect the evil and negative attitudes, feelings and actions of hopelessness, greed, disrespect, dishonour and disunity at no point in time

LIFE has no meaning if you're not seeking and serving truth and honour as the top and highest priority.

LIFE is never about any make believe bullshit. It's always about Good conquering evil and Love triumphing over hate.

It's all about having manners, love, respect and good intentions for one another, if you're enjoying one day at a time.

LIFE teaches that beauty is only skin deep. It's ageless and never a treacherous mental and spiritual journey.

It's all about displaying godly qualities in the battle of good intentions over evil spirits at all times.

It's not complicated if everyone has the Creators original plan as their guiding light and follows the laws of creation to the fullest.

LIFE is about showing honesty, integrity and giving thanks to the Creator for the Breath of fresh air.

LIFE is all about letting your lamp of truth, honour and loyalty shine bright on a daily basis.

It's never about supporting and promoting hopelessness, greed, disrespect, dishonour, and disunity at no point in time.

LIFE is the glue that keeps the Creators original plan and the laws of creation from ever falling apart.

It's never involved with any collaboration with evil and negative spirits, but mental and spiritual relapse just would not let us go.

LIFE is all about conforming to reality.

LIFE has no substitute for it.

LIFE.

ALL RIGHTS RESERVED
July 23, 2013
Read on The Avalanche Radio Show on 08/12/2013

NEWS FLASH
By
Mr. Dave R. Queeley

IT'S REALITY COMING ACROSS THE WIRE!

The Ourstory Recorder aka The V. I. Hit Factory has got it and has figured it out. L.E.A.C. aka **L**evelized **E**nergy **A**djustment **C**lause is an excuse by Joe Bogus aka the government to pay its W.A.P.A. bill, so the sufferers keep on suffering. Joe Bogus is now using L.E.A.C. like a pimp to pay back all those millions of unpaid bills on the sweat, guts and blood of the people who are being economically oppressed on a daily basis without any end and TKO in sight. Joe Bogus is now sending the evil and negative message that no citizen can hide from L.E.A.C.

L.E.A.C. will never help with the removal of the widespread corruption that is now going on in Joe Bogus every single day that goes by because W.A.P.A. is finally getting paid. It's no secret that Joe Bogus has not paid its bills for decades; so they had to find a way to pay it back. It's a damn shame they are using L.E.A.C. to do that without any end, TKO and solution in sight for miles; while the people continue to be oppressed on a daily basis. L.E.A.C. has caused so many businesses to go out of business because their electricity bill was too damn high to pay every month. That means many people have lost their jobs and things are looking and getting worse every single day that goes by.

L.E.A.C. is a completely unjustified and shameful act by Joe Bogus because it's an affront to equal rights and justice for the people who are being oppressed on a daily basis by injustice and darkness. We the People have not made the positive, moderate and courageous contribution to the ongoing positive discussion of when are we going to arrest L.E.A.C. and its pimp for continually sucking the blood and life out of those who are not a part of the privileged few aka poor people; who do not have the ka-ching aka money to pay up or keep greasing the wheels of injustice and darkness. L.E.A.C. is a firestorm that has engulfed the people who are not a part of the privileged few. The **L**evelized **E**nergy **A**djustment **C**lause needs to be on an indefinite leave of absence from these people's W.A.P.A. bill A.S.A.P.

L.E.A.C. is now operating like the terrorist group called al-Qaida that needs to be bombed every day until they do not exist anymore in Creation. The scumbags who are in charge and working for Joe Bogus who has given the **L**evelized **E**nergy **A**djustment **C**lause the power to operate with impunity have been disinterested with the details of politics and civic administration which is never on their mind, so they leave many of those decision making matters to injustice and darkness. This is not good news for the people being oppressed on a daily basis without any end and TKO in sight. L.E.A.C. can now be put in the class of all those first degree robberies of the past like ENRON,

TYCO and WORLDCOM; believe it or not. L.E.A.C. will never put the people in a situation where they will be and feel comfortable mentally and spiritually, opening their W.A.P.A. bill. L.E.A.C. is now a top-notch criminal enterprise that some people say will soon pass the mafia in notarization as an organized crime family. It's ungodly and unfair to the people on so many different levels that it's now a killer headache and there are no pills that can stop this pain.

The **L**evelized **E**nergy **A**djustment **C**lause is now the street version of Billy the Kid or Bonnie and Clyde, it's now enjoying a very charmed and illustrious career as a shot caller aka boss player. L.E.A.C. does more harm than good to the people who are being oppressed on a daily basis without any end, TKO and solution in sight. It keeps the electrical massacres alive that has spread to every part of our communities and neighbourhoods all over Creation. This message aka word sound NEWS FLASH is another fine documentation that L.E.A.C. is a bolt of lightning from injustice and darkness that only helps keep the people in electrical slavery as they move forward deeper into the century of the unknown.

The lack of progress by Joe Bogus is a big problem because, it's just a lack of will that keeps Joe bogus from doing what's right or the hard work of solving and fixing all social ills, problems and conflicts that L.E.A.C. continues to cause on a daily basis. It reflects the politically poisonous atmosphere of Greed is good and hatred who are the offsprings of injustice and darkness.

The people who are not a part of the privileged few aka poor people now need a grass roots activism that will compel these people to take a more forceful and powerful stand against the shot caller aka boss player now called L.E.A.C. once and for all. In the 21st century, no one rich or poor is immune or exempt from the hardship and psychological trauma that L.E.A.C. continues to cause for no good reason under the sun, moon and stars.

L.E.A.C. is now a first class gold digger and could care less if the people live or die, just as long as they get paid every month. It's a cruel reminder that things will never get better if this electrical monopoly continues to happen while Joe Bogus continues to look the other way or turn a blind eye to what's going on in our communities and neighbourhoods every single day that goes by. The people who are not a part of the privileged few aka W.A.P.A. bill continue to give them a black eye every time they open up the envelope. L.E.A.C. is now like a stranger living in their house who has no conflict resolution on their mind. They continue to prepare the way for the arrival of SELF destruction and death of the people who are not a part of the privileged few.

It's now in a different orbit entirely from Good over Evil at all times. The people who are in charge and working for Joe Bogus needs to be charged with first degree aiding and abetting the enemy who continues to commit crimes against humanity for helping L.E.A.C. continuous slaughtering of the people who are being oppressed on a daily basis . The **L**evelized **E**nergy **A**djustment **C**lause now has similarities and methods that seems like it is a dictator. We the People best believe it; L.E.A.C. was put in place to wipe us out economically.

THE END OF REALITY ON THE WIRE!

ALL RIGHTS RESERVED
09/27/2014

Books also written by Dave Queeley

The Truth Is Guaranteed

Let The Truth Be Told

The Truth Is Freedom

The Truth In Evil Never Sleeps

Put It Down

FIND THESE BOOKS ON AMAZON.COM/BOOKS

Made in the USA
Columbia, SC
29 October 2024